Ecological
GARDENING

Ecological
GARDENING

Sally Cunningham

THE CROWOOD PRESS

First published in 2009 by
The Crowood Press Ltd
Ramsbury, Marlborough
Wiltshire SN8 2HR

www.crowood.com

British Library Cataloguing-in-Publication Data
A catalogue record for this book is available from the British Library.

ISBN 978 1 84797 125 8

Illustrations by Caroline Pratt

Frontispiece: Rhoda Nottridge

Thanks to the following people and organizations for allowing their gardens, pets and children to be photographed for this book: Achamore Gardens, Isle of Gigha; Belgrave Hall Museum, Leicester; Garden Organic, Ryton Organic Gardens; Gwyneth and Paul Yerrington; Jenny and Graham Cousins; Linda and Martin Goddard; Lynette Jones; Maureen and Mick Falkner; Morris Williamson; Newarke Houses Museum, Leicester; Rosemary Bradley; the allotment holders at Croft, Groby, Redhill and Saffron Lane; the gardeners of Bradford-on-Avon, Croft and Stoney Stanton; Waterperry Gardens

DEDICATION
To my parents

Typeset by Servis Filmsetting Ltd, Stockport, Cheshire
Printed and bound in Malaysia by Times Offset (M) Sdn Bhd

Contents

What is ecologically aware gardening?

With increasing changes in our climate and knowledge that we have limited resources, more and more people want to do their best for the wider world. As financial, climatic and political problems grow worldwide, the necessity of growing what we can at home and using what we grow to help elsewhere in the garden becomes ever more important.

Ecologically aware gardening is about recognizing that even small actions can have big impacts on our lives and those of other creatures around us, and therefore adapting our actions to limit our effects on the rest of the world. It means realizing that not everybody can have the ideal garden, even if they have the best of intentions, and it aims to help you make the most of what you've got in terms of time, money and space.

Ecological gardening also means using the minimum of extras, avoiding use of artificial chemicals, and reusing or recycling wherever possible.

Gardening sustainably means adapting your garden to its site – you will have to sacrifice the habits of gardeners who always want to grow heathers on chalk soils or carnations in a peat bog! Grow plants which are naturally happy with the conditions where you live. Recognizing your soil's limitations and learning to see them as advantages is just part of becoming more earth-conscious.

If we can all make slight changes in how we garden, the combined effect will have a far greater significance than creating another national nature reserve. Attracting wildlife to your patch of earth isn't difficult: it could be making as insignificant a change as growing single annual flowers instead of doubles, for instance, or planting a native or near-native tree instead of an alien species, or letting a few parsnips run to seed on an allotment.

This Acer *is growing exactly where it should, in a woodland setting.*

By composting garden and food waste, leaves, paper and cardboard, we can reduce the amount we send to landfill while enriching our soils. Collecting rainwater provides better supplies for plants than tapwater: the amount of energy needed to purify water to drinkable quality makes it a wicked waste to just use it for irrigation.

Ideally don't have any paving so you don't park the car on it at all! But as real life isn't like this, use permeable paving which helps the soil retain rain, instead of hard standing which sheds water very rapidly and can result in flash floods.

Rather than buying masses of bedding plants, destined to be thrown out at the end of the year, raise your own from seed or cuttings and use them for a few select container displays. Could you achieve equal effects by planting hardy perennials or a self-seeding annual mixture instead?

As gardens shrink, use a push-powered mower and edging shears to tend the lawn, saving energy used for powered equipment and keeping you fit. Where there is a genuine need for power, try to use solar panels to drive fountains, garden or even shed lighting, and other garden machinery, from lawnmowers to mole repellents.

The most important part of becoming ecologically aware is to be in tune with your garden. Realize that you don't have to chase some impossible dream of perfection: living things develop illnesses from time to time, and have periods when they're just not at their best, exactly as we do. Equally, there will be intervals of true delight as everything grows unexpectedly, suddenly splendid.

Whatever your garden, at some times of year it will demand more attention than others. Garden work is part of the natural cycle of the year as much as the appearance of bees. Rediscovering seasonal rhythms is all part of listening to the pulse of the earth.

CHAPTER 1

Designing an eco-garden

What should be in an ecologically sustainable garden? What can your garden contribute to helping the world?

Well, it all depends on your site, soil and time available – but like all gardens, there should be a few essentials: compost, water, food and flowers – and all the other little things which you want a garden to do, but not necessarily look at.

Think about what you want to do in your garden – a place to sit out, away from the neighbours? A space to entertain? Your own green sanctuary, or just somewhere the children can play?

To misquote William Morris, you should have nothing in your garden which is not useful or beautiful or which stands no chance of growing well.

If you move to a different garden, you will probably be fired with great enthusiasm and see all sorts of ways you could improve the existing plantings, grow more food or save water. Sadly, this enthusiasm often expires as you encounter unforeseen problems elsewhere, and leaves you feeling disillusioned with your growing ability, while the garden looks worse than when you started.

It's always better to do something to improve your green growing than to do nothing, even if this means taking what seems an inordinately long time to do it. A good rule of thumb is to do very little to established areas of plants for the first twelve months in a new garden (you'll probably be very busy working on improvements inside anyway) and simply watch what emerges, because you may otherwise destroy hidden treasures.

If you're too impatient to do this, then at least try to identify things before slashing them down. Some plants, like the infamous stag's horn sumach, *Rhus typhina*, are best left undisturbed,

simply because they will resprout again and again from the smallest particle of root.

DESIGN BASICS

Even if you only have a roof garden, you should allocate space for two compost containers – one to fill while the other one is maturing. In a really tiny space these could be as simple as a pair of substantial boxes (for example recycled polystyrene fish boxes) with homemade plywood lids.

You'll need a method of capturing rainwater, and should allocate space for at least one water-butt. This is a genuine necessity, in these days of increasing prices for metered water.

If you have a vehicle, where should it live? Most councils demand off-street car parking, certainly in the larger towns and cities, but you shouldn't pave over the entire front garden, because of its contribution to flash flooding. Bicycles need secure, ideally dry, storage, along with kit to maintain them, and there's rarely enough room indoors. You'll also need somewhere to keep garden tools, flowerpots or children's toys...

Lastly, being practical, you need somewhere to store rubbish and recycling bins, and a washing line or rotary clothes dryer is a must...plus somewhere to sit as well!

After all these demands on your precious garden space, is there going to be any room for plants? The answer has to be yes, but you will need to be very selective – or very keen and hard-working – to keep from overcrowding the garden.

When looking at a garden new to you, it's very hard to visualize what you want to put in place with what you see. If there already are many

Willow seat with a cushion of chamomile makes a self-perpetuating fragrant bower.

MAIN POINTS FOR AN ECO-GARDEN

1. Use reclaimed or recycled materials throughout for your hard landscaping – brick, slabs, stone, timber. Acceptable materials include industrial by-products such as slate chippings, glass cullet or mill waste (in preference to gravel) or made from renewable resources such as terracotta or brick. If reclaimed timber is unavailable, ensure it's come from a renewable, ideally local, source – look for the FSE (Federation for a Sustainable Environment) logo, or the one for a Tropical Sustainable Timber (and make sure you know where it was grown). Renewable choice examples would be red cedar, European larch or green oak rather than teak, or coppiced hazel and ash poles rather than bamboo, unless it's home grown. Alternatively use one of the many 'woodlook' products made from recycled plastic.

2. Always make provision for other creatures (birds, bees, butterflies, beneficial insects) by including food sources such as flowers or berries, water and shelter. Include some native species in permanent plantings.

3. Reduce food miles by including some edible plants or a fruit tree wherever possible. Growing your own food not only makes you feel good and more connected to the earth, it's healthy too – maximum freshness means highest levels of nutrients and vitamins.

4. Always have a composting area. Compost whatever you can and use your compost regularly. If circumstances mean you can't compost for any reason, try to make sure your waste goes to a municipal composting area.

5. Save water wherever possible in the garden by appropriate planting and water collection. Mulch exposed soil to retain moisture wherever practicable.

6. Reduce electricity use by making space for a clothes line or rotary dryer wherever possible. Use solar sources for garden lighting, pond pumps and other garden power uses wherever practicable. Be inventive!

7. Grow the right plants for the site. Don't plant anything where you know it will always be unhappy. If something you thought should grow fails, before trying something different, research further until you find what really likes growing there.

established plants, it can be even harder to imagine your replacement plants than mentally populating a bare lawn.

Look first at what you have. Your choice of plants will be decided mostly by soil and site, so finding out more about what's there is vital before you make final decisions.

Where are you? If the garden is at the base of a slope, it may be in a frost-pocket, or prone to flooding, while higher on the top of a hill the drainage will be good but the site may need protection from vicious winds. Steep slopes lend themselves to terraces, while super-soggy sites are going to need raised areas for paths and maybe beds as well, unless you want only bog-garden plants.

Is your soil clay, sandy or are you lucky enough to have the ideal, a lovely loam? Whatever the soil is like, it is capable of improvement by good husbandry: applications of compost, using mulches and careful cultivations, will all help develop a deep, rich tilth over time.

PAVING AND HARD SURFACES

Paths and patios may need to be laid, if they're not already in place – do you want to use recycled slabs, bark or gravel (both of which will need constant renewal and an edging)? Or possibly brick

Laying recycled granite cobbles with plenty of space between them leaves room for thyme to grow in the gaps.

Beside a row of chives, a garden path made from chipped bark will stand considerable wear without becoming muddy in wet weather.

paving? A lightweight and long-lasting alternative is wood or stone look-alike recycled plastic, or a mixture of recycled plastic and rubber, which is very durable, rot resistant and reasonably priced.

Although they are so familiar, concrete and cement products are now not considered to be sustainable, generating vast volumes of CO_2 in their manufacture and should be avoided if possible. The process of manufacture is complex, beginning with mining and mechanically pulverizing rock, heating limestone to very high temperatures (releasing its stored CO_2) and subsequent mixing and casting, before transporting heavy loads long-distance.

Brick, on the other hand, is more planet friendly, as although the clay has to be open-cast mined and baked in its manufacture, this is less energy demanding, and much less carbon is generated than equivalent quantities of cement. If laid in contact with wet soil, household or common bricks, being porous, will break down in a few years, so only engineering, hard or 'blue' brick should be used for paths.

An alternative to gravel or brick is a self-bonding grit and silt mixture (sometimes known as hoggin), a naturally occurring rock formation which is mined in several parts of the UK. This is very long-lasting, and drains well in heavy rain. For maximum life it should be compacted using a mechanically vibrating plate. Like other stone-based products it can be kept weed-free by use of a flame gun.

When you have to park a car on top of paving or any other hard standing, remember you will need at least 12in (30cm) of hardcore below the penultimate layer of sand or fine grit, before you place the first slab or membrane on top. If you have to remove this amount of soil, can you use it in other areas of the garden, for example to create raised beds?

Many local authorities now demand permeable paving for car-parking areas, rather than concrete or tarmac which causes rapid rainwater run-off which the sewers can't cope with, thus contributing to flash flooding. Before installing this, check that the area where you intend to use it is well above the normal water table level and the soil type is suitable. Some soils, such as very heavy clays or ultra-light sands, can become unfit to carry heavy loads in extremely wet conditions.

An important consideration is how you will maintain the hard landscaping after it's been installed – weed control and removal of fallen debris are major work over a large area, and all surfaces have their advantages or disadvantages. Weeds can be suppressed by laying a semi-permeable plastic membrane before installing paving or bark, but windblown seedlings will always present problems at some times of the year. Hoeing will work well on bark or gravel paths, if done regularly, but can be laborious, as well as time consuming. Plastic, rubber and bark can't be flameweeded, for obvious reasons.

Plants will grow in all sorts of unexpected places, if you choose the right species, such as this Eschscholzia californica *happily rooting in a limestone wall.*

Paths made from bark or loose stone need edgings, to keep their material in place. If you have a small area, you can use recycled bricks or tiles, but these are quite expensive. Wood is a cheaper edging, and looks more appropriate if combined with bark. Avoid using old railway sleepers, which have been impregnated with tar, as this is a potential carcinogen. Untreated sleepers are now offered for sale from wood yards and architectural salvage agents, as are reclaimed wooden beams which are sub-standard for weight bearing in building use but make perfectly good path edging. Young conifer plantation thinnings were formerly very cheap and the trunks were often used for path edgings, giving an attractive rustic appearance and taking a long time to decay because of their high resin content. As biomass has become more popular as a fuel, these sadly are becoming scarce, but it's always worth consulting your local parks department or small landowners to see if they may be felling a few odd-shaped saplings which you can use.

ABOVE: *Engineering brick is ideal for creating complex designs.*

LEFT: *Coarsely broken slate chippings contrast with the texture of smooth white birch stems.*

LAWN OR MEADOW?

Lawns can be bare, barren areas for wildlife, biologically sterile regions of monoculture or sweeping swathes of restful green, depending on your view. A slightly less than perfect, mildly weedy lawn can still look good, and is a useful wildife area as well as pleasing to the eye.

Most gardeners will still want a lawn to sit on or set off the rest of the planting, and provided it's not too intensively kept there's no reason why not: after all, rabbit- or sheep-grazed turf is a natural habitat, even if it's richer in species than your average back garden.

Try to use a push mower every few days, at least on smaller grassy areas, rather than a powered one, to diminish your carbon emissions. Good push mowers are hard to find: manufacturers please take note. (However, since writing this, a good push mower has become available via the Organic Catalogue, *see* Useful Addresses on page 126.) For pocket handkerchief lawns, you could even use a few guinea-pigs in a portable run, which live contentedly in single-sex groups and can trim down grass to bowling green standards. They'll need moving daily and will give you a well fed if slightly patchwork lawn. Robotic automatic lawnmowers topped with solar cells can be set to mow continuously if you want the silent mechanical equivalent, but they aren't cheap and won't fertilize the grass either.

GRASS CUTTING

Cutting methods vary according to the season.

In spring, grass grows swiftly and is relatively soft, but can be damaged by night frosts if cut too closely, so trim little and often. Heavy dews encourage fungal growth if cuttings are allowed to remain on the newly shorn grass overnight, so collect the mowings and use them as nitrogen feed for the compost heap.

Drier weather and longer days in summer mean that the grass growth slows, so shorter mowings can be left on the lawn to dry, acting as a replenishing mulch.

As autumn approaches the days shorten, and leaves fall, blocking light and air to grass below. Set the mower higher to collect a mixture of cut leaves and grass, which will decompose quicker than leaves alone but will be just as valuable.

During the winter mow only if the grass continues to grow on rare sunny days, when the mower won't skid or scalp the soil. Keep off the grass if at all possible when it's frozen, as this is when most damage is caused.

Always use the right blend of grass seed for your site: most seed companies will offer at least a shady, play and fine lawn selection.

Wildflower meadows were all the rage a few years ago, but sadly for those of us who have relatively small back gardens, they are not really practical. They're really difficult to maintain on a small scale where the garden has to do other things than just look pretty, as they won't stand being walked on when in flower, and rely on impoverished soil with regular grazing rather than lawn mowing to control both flowering time and height of growth.

Some wildflowers are almost bound to find themselves in the lawn, regardless: white clover (*Trifolium repens*) in dry areas, selfheal (*Prunella vulgaris*) where it's damp and germander speedwell (*Veronica chamaedrys*) with brilliant blue eyes that flourish in grass almost anywhere in sun. If they become too advanced, hand-weed with a

daisy grubber, or simply alter the mowing regime: mowing too low can weaken the grass, so set the height a little higher and mow more often to weaken the weeds instead. Clover fixes nitrogen as well as feeding the bees – if you can, try to live with

A mixture of wildflowers growing in their natural habitat.

a flower-studded lawn. If you have trees growing from the grass, set the mower slightly higher underneath them, to create shadows of daisy, hop trefoil and speedwell flowers lighting up the turf like stars.

Rather than go for a full-blown wildflower meadow, if you have average soil it's better to grow a few wildflowers in a single area where the soil is particularly poor, or simply blend in some of the more attractive annual species in the borders. Annual or cornfield meadow mixtures are more suited to gardens, being weeds of cultivated ground, and can be scattered anywhere you haven't made up your mind about yet. Rather than go for a purely all-native species selection, choose a pictorial meadow mixture which will give a longer flowering period. Prepare the seedbed in late summer or early spring before sowing. Autumn sowings will give an earlier flowering, taller display.

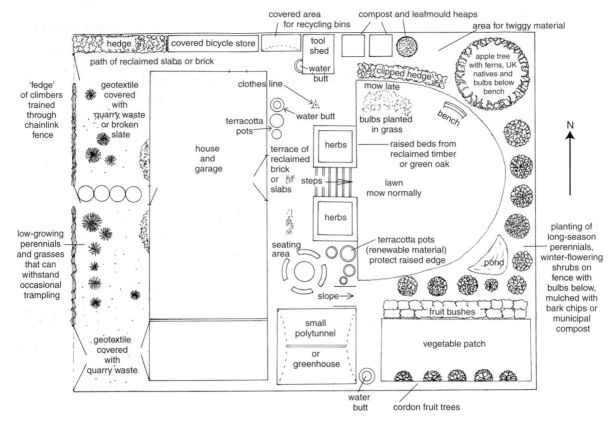

Suggested plan for an eco-garden for a suburban couple with no children.

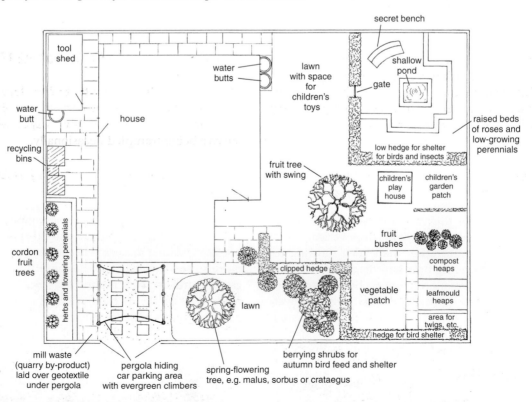

Suggested plan for a suburban family eco-garden.

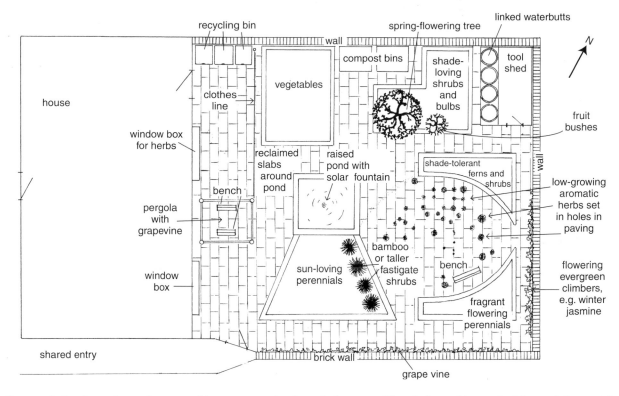

Suggested plan for an inner city terraced house eco-garden for a single person. The whole yard is paved with recycled material, e.g. engineering brick or recycled slabs.

In the early stages when planning a meadow, make sure you mark out a defined path or set out stepping stones for access or you may find it's not so much wildflowers you're cultivating as very happy but not so attractive weeds.

In an ideal world, something like this would be the perfect playground for every child…

GARDENS WITH CHILDREN

Children will always play football or leave toys on the lawn. This is fine, but you will need to plan resilient shrubs near the lawn edges which can survive being trampled occasionally.

…but these recycled tractor tyres can be a good substitute to leap, climb and jump about on.

Be imaginative in recycling when it comes to playthings. Well-washed, heavy duty food containers or catering-size plastic tubs, buried open edge down, three-quarters deep in the ground, will act as drums or stepping stones, lasting for several years.

Large sections of branched tree-trunk, or a basic 4 × 4in (10 × 10cm) wooden frame, securely embedded in the ground can provide a simple climbing frame or den base. Don't be tempted to use tanalized timber, which contains a number of heavy-metal nasties – provided it's sufficiently thick, untreated hardwood rots very slowly. If you are lucky enough to find a source of oak, plum or yew boughs, they take a long time to decay, due to resins or tannins in the wood, so persist in good condition for ages even in a garden where they are always in contact with damp soil. Branches from trees which have been deliberately felled when in good health are preferable to those which have just dropped off of their own accord, which may have some invisible internal defect.

Every child loves a tree-house, and if you have a large tree in the garden this may be a possibility: ideally, to hold it up, build an independently supported platform which isn't secured to the tree itself. Avoid wood chafing with the tree trunk if possible, to allow the tree to move in winds independently of the platform. Make sure you talk to your immediate neighbours before constructing a tree-house, as some people can object to suddenly being overlooked.

Mature trees can also be the supports for swings

Growing potatoes is always a great way to grab a child's interest in gardening.

and other apparatus, from rope ladders to hammocks. As a safety guideline, check if the rope and branch will support the weight of two adults before releasing the kids! For the tree's sake, use a thicker, rather than thinner rope, and check it every few months for both security of knotting (always use reef, not slip, knots) and tightness on the tree. Plaited nylon cord is usually cheapest and longest lasting: look for new ropes from a supplier of canal boat fittings, farm suppliers or ships' chandlers. If you want to be totally green, you can use hemp or jute ropes, which are biodegradable, but be aware they don't last so long, and they often stretch more with use.

A child will probably need to be about four or five years old before they can take an active role in growing plants, although they will have great fun helping out before this, and can be introduced to large, easy-to-handle subjects such as planting potatoes, onion sets or well-established seedlings in modules. Don't be upset if they want to dig holes rather than cultivate – they will be learning valuable lessons about soil structure, elementary physics and mechanics even if it just looks as if they're getting covered in mud.

GARDENS FOR ADULTS

For the harassed commuter, a low-labour garden is a must, so the planting should be permanent and perennial rather than all annuals or container based. You may want to concentrate on night-flowering plants, to prolong the limited time you can spend outdoors on long summer evenings or to enjoy their perfume drifting in when you come home.

With careful choices you can limit garden work to simple removal of old plant material once a season and the occasional weeding, with plant division every five years or so to renew their vigour. If you have hardly any free time, and just want a lawn with a tree in, choose a fruit tree so that at least your one plant can be productive, and allow the edges of the lawn to be slightly longer, growing into hedge bases if possible, to allow space for invertebrates and birds.

Older gardeners may appreciate a warm sunny

FLOWERS FROM THE NIGHT GARDEN

Nowadays with so many people having such busy lives, the only chance to sit out in the garden and relax is often near the end of the daylight. By summer sundown, most day living butterflies and birds have retired to their nests but the nightshift is just about to emerge from the shadows...so light a citronella candle or apply a little insect repellent and just watch.

Ponds are great centres of late night insect activity, quite apart from their midge and mosquito potential – you may be surprised to find water boatmen, *Corixa punctata*, flying vigorously at night, feeding on newly emerging flies.

White flowers show up best in twilight, like this Nigella.

You will probably see more moths – and bats if you're lucky – if your garden contains night-bloomers such as the biennial sweet rocket, summer jasmine or night-scented stocks, which perfume the air to advertise their late-night nectar. Placing fragrant, open-faced flowers near to garden lighting also helps. Try to minimize light pollution by having switches on solar lights, so that when you're indoors they're switched off.

Fragrant Evening Flowering Plants

- Bladder campion (*Silene vulgaris*)
- *Brugmansia spp*
- Cherry Pie (*Heliotropum x hybridum*)
- Common Jasmine (*Jasminum officinale*)
- Confederate or Star Jasmine (*Trachlospermum asiaticum*)
- Evening Primrose (*Oenothera biennis*)
- Honeysuckle (*Lonicera spp*)
- Lilies (esp. species and oriental types)
- Night scented Stock (*Matthiola bicornis*)
- Petunias (particularly double or dark coloured shades)
- Soapwort (*Saponaria officinalis*)
- Sweet Rocket (*Hesperis matronalis*)
- Tobacco plant (*Nicotiana spp and hybrids*)

Summer moths are as punctual in their emergence as swallows, each species arriving in turn. Their favourite foods include red valerian, petunias and lavender, where their long tongues can easily reach down into the nectaries.

On long summer evenings, bees will work overtime to visit Asclepias *for nectar.*

area to sit out in – and so will the butterflies. Plant nectar-rich flowers with simple open faces, and just enjoy watching who visits. Just because the gardener is elderly does not mean that their growing days should stop – but obviously the older one becomes, the less energy is available.

Raised vegetable or alpine beds at table-top height make growing vegetables or flowers much easier for those in a wheelchair. When constructing brick raised beds leave drainage gaps at least a quarter brick wide in the lower courses to provide desirable residences for amphibians and predatory beetles, which happily munch on slugs. Micro-irrigation systems can be installed, complete with solar powered pumps to make watering less taxing.

Sloping paths rather than steps, laid out with gentle turns rather than sharp right-angles make wheeling barrows easier for those with ageing joints. Recycled ridged stable blocks provide

Simple green shade is refreshing for mind and body.

securer footing than plain slabs, which can easily become slippery with algae during the winter.

Weeding is not eliminated but can be made less of a chore when a permeable membrane has been laid over the growing area, with holes for planting shrubs or perennials to grow through it. A mulch of coarse bark chippings (which will need periodic renewal) will look attractive and require limited maintenance. It'll also be an instant home for beetles, centipedes and other beneficial insects, unlike gravel or polished pebbles, which are less attractive for invertebrates. Bark chippings can cope with light traffic from wheelbarrows or feet without becoming treacherous in wet weather.

THE PROTECTED ENVIRONMENT

A greenhouse or small polytunnel can be a very attractive feature for gardeners of all ages, being somewhere to potter out of the weather, as well as a valuable resource for prolonging the growing season or protecting plants over winter. Heating is not essential, as winter wet can be a bigger plant killer than cold. Extra insulation can be added by a layer of horticultural fleece or bubble-wrap or may be integral to the design. In the excellent (if not cheap) Keder house, heavily insulated clear sliding

panels are pulled into place during winter and replaced with netting during the summer giving the home grower the best part of both worlds.

Removable benches can be made using folding tables or planks supported on simple trestles, to maximize the growing area in spring when seedlings can be raised at higher levels, and removed or folded away for summer when the floor space can be devoted to growing crops. Whatever size greenhouse, try to incorporate a folding chair – it's much more comfortable doing fiddly, time-consuming work, such as pricking out, when seated.

If you are tempted to buy a second hand glasshouse, you will almost certainly need to replace most, if not all, of the glass. Horticultural glass is thinner than ordinary window glass, so is cheaper in price, but not by as much as you might expect.

Rigid polythene or perspex panels are sometimes recommended instead as a safety measure, but if you choose these instead of glass, remember that they will deteriorate with age, often becoming opaque. Another factor in favour of glass is that it has better thermal capacity – a greenhouse with

A greenhouse 6ft x 8ft/2m x 2.6m will be large enough for most back gardens, for raising cuttings and half-hardy seedlings in. Remember to allow space for rain water collection, with easy access to the water butts.

glass windows retains heat better after a winter night than one with plastic panels. However, domestic glass recyclers rarely accept horticultural glass, which leaves breakages to go to landfill – not very green!

Second hand polytunnel frames are a good investment, if all the pieces are included, as these can last for many years. The plastic film should last for at least three, if not five growing seasons, unless you are in a very exposed area, but remember to install anti-hot spot tape on the top surfaces of the frame, as these areas can overheat, causing plastic to distort or melt in hot weather. If you contact polytunnel specialists, for a small extra cost you can purchase special plastic films which can reduce disease, condensation or encourage vegetative growth rather than flowering. Many of these firms will accept old polytunnel film for recycling, or it can be disposed of at the municipal recycling area.

Polytunnels, and to a lesser extent greenhouses should always be placed in a sheltered area, with the shorter end facing the prevailing winds.

Those adopting a DIY approach to making your own greenhouse or tunnel should bear in mind that some plastics exude chemicals which are toxic to plants, especially when they are heated – so invest in horticultural film rather than any clear plastic you can obtain.

If you haven't got room for a conventional greenhouse, there are a variety of innovative designs which use very little floor space, or you could improvise a lean-to construction against the house wall.

Remember that if you grow a large number of plants from seed in your greenhouse, you will probably want a coldframe to harden them off in. As a personal opinion, if I had the choice between only having a large coldframe, or just a small greenhouse, I'd go for the frame every time, using windowsills to start off tender seedlings.

A large drawer, painted with yacht varnish inside and out (keeping it waterproof so the wood will last) topped with an old windowframe or a layer of plastic sheeting can make a very good DIY coldframe for little or no outlay, and it's always worth looking for whatever else you can improvise. Roll-top hairdressing fittings, discarded salad trays from fridges and even clear plastic computer keyboard covers are all examples of things I've seen pressed into use for providing extra protection for tender seedlings on allotments and back gardens.

SHEDS, SCREENS AND FENCES

Every gardener, if not every garden, needs a shed: if appropriately designed, these can become a garden feature rather than something to be tucked away. Sheds are sanctuaries for all sorts of wildlife as well as gardeners! Sheds collect water from their roofs, and act as a windbreak and as a storage heater to nurture susceptible plants when they release heat trapped in their timbers overnight, so site your shed where it will be most useful. Will you want to site solar panels on it to power a pond pump, for example?

'Green roofs' which slow down water runoff, and give you an additional growing area make an attractive feature for a shed, but are heavier than the more usual tarpaper. As a rough guideline, a 6 × 4ft (2 × 1.2m) shed will need corner posts 3 × 2in (8 × 5cm) and walls of a minimum thickness of ¾in (2cm) marine plywood when using a green roof with 2½in (6cm) of gravel, 1in (2.5cm) of substrate, and a layer of butyl liner for waterproofing is to be added to the normal roof. Suitable plants for this depth of gravel would be succulent species such as *Sedums, Crassulas, Sempervirum* or *Saxifrage spp.*

If you live next to a busy road or with something you wish to disguise in the garden, some sort of hedge or screen is very important. Growing plants filter pollution and reduce wind speeds and noise. As permanent structures, unlike timber fence panels or stone walls, they only need planting once, apart from any aesthetic advantages. Hedges can frame a scene or conceal a new part of the garden from immediate gaze, as well as separate you from the neighbours.

Whatever you plant for hedging, ensure that there's an ample gap between the hedge and any growing plants. You will need to reach the hedge to clip it, possibly with a step-ladder, and the dry root zone close to the base will make anything growing next to it perform poorly. A yard/metre

Sheds can be pretty, potty or practical.

between a hedge and border is not too much.

For a hedge 6ft (2m) high and 18in (50cm) wide, of a species which only needs to be cut back once annually, expect to have to compost or shred at least three barrow loads of prunings every yard/metre in length. Is your composting area big enough?

Other screening materials include relatively expensive hurdles, which will last around eight years with care. Buying hurdles gives employment to a craftsman: making your own is quite possible, but heavy on the arms, and after trying you'll appreciate how much work goes into just a single panel.

Making Hurdles

If you want to try DIY, use oak or green split sweet chestnut poles for the uprights and long unbranched hazel strips or willow withies to weave between. Thread the long pieces in and out between the uprights, bend at the ends through 180 degrees (you may need to use a mallet to help the wood bend or cut it halfway with secaturs, depending on the wood used), then repeat the process. Batt the woven stuff as far down the uprights as possible with a mallet, to allow for shrinkage as the wood dries to keep the finished hurdle tight.

Simple brushwood or bamboo screens can also be made or bought, and are less substantial, with a lifespan of about three years at most. Recycled

Hurdles are traditionally made from hazel, as shown here, but other woods such as willow, birch or elm have been used in the past.

plastic strips can be manufactured to appear very like bamboo and are somewhat costlier, but longer lasting.

A 'fedge' is often the ideal solution when space is limited – it's a very thin structure, something between a fence and a hedge. Fedges may be as simple as a chain link fence covered with ivy or winter jasmine, or a more elaborate structure made from willow. Willow fedges and other structures are becoming more popular, but need careful placing. The trees are vigorous, demanding a damp site or moisture retentive soil to thrive, and during summer, when they should be left unpruned, take up a large space, at least 3ft (1m) either side. Willows generally, particularly the rapid young growth encouraged by hard pruning, are food for the large willow aphid, which in turn attracts wasps, who feed on their honeydew, and consequently willow structures, particularly long tunnels with no ready means of escape, are not always suitable for children.

GREEN ROOFING

Green roofing is becoming increasingly popular for garden outbuildings and garages, making a valuable asset for wildlife, even in small areas. These are usually built up of thin layers of gravel or a fine sand base planted with drought tolerant species such as sedums laid over a waterproof layer or membrane. Alternatively a deeper substrate can be laid, which allows up to 12in (30cm) of root depth, and seeds scattered to create a self-perpetuating plant community.

A green roof, particularly the deeper version, requires stronger walls to support the extra weight, but these need not be very much different from the normal buildings on a small scale if using sedums or similar shallow rooted species. In exposed regions, green roofs for sheds can anchor them better by providing extra stability in strong winds. Green roofs should be almost flat or slightly angled, with no more than 40 degrees of slope, or the gravel will tend to slip to the eaves. Guttering is still needed,

An example of drought-tolerant species suitable for a shallow green roof.

MAKING WILLOW STRUCTURES

In the right place woven willow can be both beautiful and a successful screen.

To build a simple woven willow fedge, you will need at least two people and a quantity of both one-year-old long willow withies (unrooted straight shoots, at least 6ft (2m) tall, cut from the previous season's growth) and hazel or ash rods about 4ft (1.3m) long to act as upright supports. Work can be done whenever the ground is unfrozen during winter. Begin by pushing in uprights of hazel sticks at least 3ft (1m) apart along the line of the fedge, and push in willow rods about 12in (30cm) apart at a 45-degree angle, leaning right every 3ft (1m) and left for the next 3ft (1m), crossing over each other several times to create a diamond pattern. Tie in securely with string or hazel bines and continue until you reach the end, when the shoots should be snipped off vertically once they have been tied to the last upright.

Ensure good weed control by laying a 12in (30cm) wide strip of semi-permeable membrane along both sides of the fedge. The plants require no further treatment until the following autumn, except watering in dry weather and checking the ties for tightness. As soon as the leaves are starting to turn colour, remove all the current season's shoots which are not in the pattern you originally tied. If there are any dead withies remove them and replace with a long shoot from this season's growth, removing all the leaves and tying in as before.

Expect a willow structure to last between fifteen and twenty years before needing replacing.

Even small structures, like this hedgehog shelter, can have living roofs.

as although the growing plants will take up some rainfall they can't cope with heavy rain. To prevent blockages with plant debris, always make sure there's a wire filter in place before the runoff enters the downpipe.

In very dry weather plants may benefit from irrigation, but apart from occasional weeding and removal of dead material, they are maintenance free. Deep roof structures may need more in the way of weeding.

Green mat roofing, complete with plants, gravel and all, can be bought by the roll, ready to lay onto a waterproofed roof, or suitable selections of seed are sown onto an existing layer of gravel and stones. A sedum mat will have a lifespan of around thirty years. In severe winters, sedums may die off, especially on the easterly side, but left alone they will often re-seed themselves.

VERTICAL GARDENING – LIVING WALLS

In very small spaces or town gardens, where there are large areas of blank wall, often the only way is up, and climbers which can be trained vertically are always in demand.

Water and nutrients at the base of a wall are often limited, so a relatively new way of growing is vertical gardening. This involves installing a secure waterproof membrane between the building wall and the growing area, which comprises a series of compost-containing bags, versions of giant growbags, supported on a wire frame, similar to the wire gabions used to contain stones on embankments. Irrigation is provided with permanently fixed drip-feed or leakhoze pipes, often fed from a rainwater collection system. Plants are fed at weekly or monthly intervals with liquid fertilizer through the irrigation system. They need trimming every four to six weeks during the growing season and can be kept in place for over five years, when most will require renewal. Suitable species which have coped successfully with climatic extremes in Europe include vigorous species such as *Parthenocissus*, *Choisya*, *Fatsia*, *Rhododendron ponticum*, *Hedera*, *Phygelius*, *Clematis viticella*, *Lonicera spp* and *Prunus lusitanica*. Slightly less vigorous herbaceous species which are happy to grow at a permanent angle include *Primula*, *Heuchera* and *Tiarella*.

Growing methods like this have beneficial effects on the buildings concerned, reducing noise and controlling temperature. The vegetation acts as extra insulation, keeping the building as much as 6°C cooler in summer and 4°C warmer in winter. Higher humidity levels and oxygen concentrations around the building in summer make city living more comfortable, reducing the 'heat bubble' effect and indirectly making the whole landscape cooler. Wildlife is attracted to the site, and people living and working in the area enjoy a different natural view, rather than a monotonous blank wall.

On a smaller scale, for gardeners with very steep slopes and little soil to work with, a new innovation is ready-planted hessian or coir fibre growing containers, each covering an area of about a yard/metre square, which can be securely anchored by plastic cable ties to fixing points such as tent pegs secured in the slope. They grow happily after installation for several years with little or no aftercare except watering, if micro-irrigation is not fitted, and after the container has rotted away there is normally sufficient root growth to retain the plants in place.

CHAPTER 2

Gardening sustainably

What does it mean to garden sustainably? Well, it's very similar to normal gardening, but with a little more thought involved.

In an ideal world, your garden should be a self-contained unit, buying in as little as possible for fertilizer and soil improvement, only importing seeds or small offsets to increase your plant populations, and finding all the material used for plant supports or garden structures within what you grow. Little or no waste would leave the garden, as it would all be composted or used in other ways, while water would be hoarded and recycled, only requiring rainfall to keep plants growing. You would have space to grow most of your own vegetable requirements, and in good seasons produce surplus for storage over winter, which you could keep in good condition until it was needed or trade for other produce from your neighbours. However, this is only practicable if you have sufficient acreage and enough time to set things in place, as well as work on the land. 'Back to the land' has been a daydream for the majority of the British population ever since the Enclosures Acts.

The old standard of an allotment with an area of approximately 300 sq yd (250 sq m) was always intended to be able to sustain a family of four with green vegetables all year round, except potatoes – if you want to be self-sufficient in these, then at least an extra 100 sq yd (80 sq m) will be required, and it will take about 200 hours a year to keep tidy and growing profitably. Most gardens, especially around modern houses, are much smaller than this and can't provide everything you will need, let alone the aesthetics of living surrounded by fence-to-fence vegetables.

A more reasonable achievement is to be able to devote about a quarter of your garden to grow fruit and vegetables. New-build houses are designed mostly for convenience shopping, and storage areas are usually too hot or too small or both. Beneficial long-term improvements in carbon reduction come from making small changes in growing habits – they'll make as much difference to the environment as installing double-glazing does for reducing domestic fuel consumption.

What you can do in your own garden is use it sensibly. Avoid being a slave to fashion – you don't need to give a garden a makeover every other year! Select a simple hard-landscape design which you can live with, choosing a few plants to form a framework. You can vary the surroundings as you have time for or desire – after all, gardening is a growing passion.

Raising perennial plants from seed is very satisfying and enables you to select your personal favourites, but is not always essential. The one thing you really should try to do is to avoid waste, and buy plants responsibly. How far did the plant have to travel before it arrived at the place where you're buying it from? If it's a long-lived subject, transport costs make its purchase probably worthwhile. Is it likely to last long in your garden? Do you know somebody who's already growing it, and would they let you have seeds or a cutting? Make sure every new plant you buy has a place to grow before you take it home.

FOOTPRINTS IN THE WIDER WORLD

What is an environmental footprint? And what can I do about it?

Your ecological footprint is a measure of the

The cottage garden, complete with washing line and compost heap.

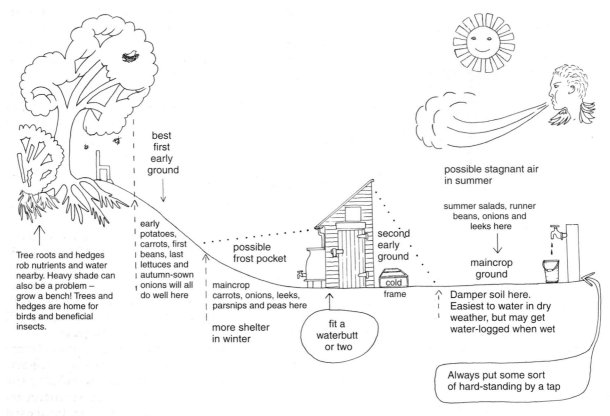

Some micro-climates on an allotment.

best first early ground

Tree roots and hedges rob nutrients and water nearby. Heavy shade can also be a problem – grow a bench! Trees and hedges are home for birds and beneficial insects.

early potatoes, carrots, first beans, last lettuces and autumn-sown onions will all do well here

possible frost pocket

maincrop carrots, onions, leeks, parsnips and peas here

more shelter in winter

fit a waterbutt or two

second early ground

cold frame

possible stagnant air in summer

summer salads, runner beans, onions and leeks here

maincrop ground

Damper soil here. Easiest to water in dry weather, but may get water-logged when wet

Always put some sort of hard-standing by a tap

total global land area which you require to fill your needs. This includes everything – the amount of land needed to grow fuel either as wood or bio diesel, as well as to build solar or wind power devices on; land for growing food and clothing; water catchment space (which may, like the wind or solar power, double up with another land use, so taking less space) and treatment area, and all other ways which keep you in your desired life-style. Whatever you do in the twenty-first century, your ecological footprint is likely to be consid-erably larger than the area of land you are cur-rently inhabiting or are responsible for. It's not easy to reduce your environmental footprint, but you should try to do what you can to conserve resources, by avoiding unnecessary waste and trying to source local products.

A carbon footprint is easier to calculate, being the amount of CO_2 that your life produces, from the long-term high carbon released from the proc-esses of cement manufacture, for example in house building and hard-landscaping products, to the much smaller but more frequent amounts given off when garden power tools such as strimmers or lawnmowers are used. Your carbon footprint is an approximate estimate of your activity on climate change and how much energy you consume.

In garden terms, there is a range of activities which have far-reaching impact on the wider world. Importing products with a long supply chain into your garden has the highest effect – this would include things like chicken manure pellets, bulky materials such as lime, commercial com-posts and horticultural plastics as well as seeds, pest control and hand tools.

Intermediate effects come from things which don't travel far but are very bulky, such as straw mulch, municipal composts or farmyard manure.

The contents of this attractive border has been raised almost exclusively from seed.

Low or very little environmental effect comes from what's homemade, such as compost, comfrey liquid and leafmould.

This is a much simplified outline, and a lot depends on what methods are used to create or distribute garden imports. For example leafmould collected by a petrol-driven leafblower from your own back garden might be less environmentally friendly than leaves gathered by a large mechanized lawnmower from a local park, because the lawnmower is more fuel efficient.

Don't feel pressured into the latest gadget, just because it's heavily promoted by a celebrity on the TV or all the neighbours have one. Hand tools have their place and are remarkably efficient. Raking up leaves is good exercise, and as you do it, savour the link with all those past gardeners who have been doing the same job every autumn for thousands of years.

GROWING FROM SEED

Buying lightweight packets of seed at first seems less problematic than buying plants. Surely things so tiny must have much less environmental impact involved in their distribution and production? Sadly, this is not always true. Keeping a strain of seed true to type is a demanding business, involving high labour costs in removing substandard or rogue plants and specialist harvesting, often spraying repeatedly with herbicides or pesticides. Seed growing is a multi-billion pound industry, and many of the most famous cultivars of common garden plants are raised in Third World countries where labour is cheap, pesticide regulation less tightly regulated and seed-drying conditions are better than the UK. When these seeds from plants grown in hot dry countries are subsequently grown in our less than perfect climate, they are often unable to cope well with the variations in the British weather. UK-raised seeds are almost always better, as they will be better adapted to our conditions. Seed which has come from organic plants, grown on an organic holding will have a built-in advantage, as it will already be naturally pre-selected for health and vigour against soil-borne pests and disease: only the strongest will have survived to set seed in the first place.

When confronted with a seed catalogue, it's easy to become overwhelmed – try to resist temptation and only order what you can reasonably grow before the seed dies of old age. The one place you know nothing will germinate is in an unopened seed packet stuck in a box somewhere. Be strong, and resist buying more than you will ever sow. If it's a cultivar you grow every year, could you save the seed yourself?

Saving Seeds

Why bother to collect, dry and winnow seeds from garden plants? It's not just about saving money, or wanting to perpetuate a favourite flower, but a small method of ensuring security for a particular patch of land. With the exception of F1 hybrids, most seeds which have self-set and germinate successfully will be those with a genetic base most likely to succeed in a specific range of conditions – so your seeds will grow better in your garden if collected from plants which have already grown there, at least for the first few generations. You can select for specific colours, heights, growth habits or time of flowering, and this is how most of our cultivars originated up until a few decades ago, when large seed companies began to employ plantbreeders.

Saving seed from home-grown vegetables is a popular method of preserving many cultivars from extinction, and has grown in popularity since the dawn of the HSL (Heritage Seed Library) in the early 1970s, when the European Union passed laws making it illegal to sell vegetable seed which was not on the National List, thus removing many old garden favourites at a stroke of the computer mouse. There is no equivalent list for flowers, but a similar organization for ornamentals would be Plant Heritage (*see* page 126). Several organizations from local organic groups to allotment or garden societies run 'Seedy Sundays' or similar swop events, usually in the winter, when members or visitors can exchange seeds.

Drying beans is best done by leaving the pods unopened, until they split by themselves.

What Seeds Can I Save?

Some plants are what are termed 'outbreeders' – they cannot self-pollinate themselves, and must exchange pollen with another flower to create viable seed embryos. The resulting seed will be genetically distinct from the parent and may look or taste very different once grown to maturity. Examples of this include all the cabbage family, from Brussels sprouts to kale; wallflowers and stocks; the cucurbits, which cross promiscuously and hybridize across species; and the primrose family, several members of which can interbreed.

Other plants are 'inbreeders' which self-fertilize

HOW LONG DOES SEED KEEP?		

These are approximations for reasonable storage times in household conditions, rather than in ideal storage.

Family	Including	Maximum storage period
Cabbage	broccoli, cauliflowers, turnips, radishes, rocket, wallflowers and Brompton stocks	5 years
Beetroot	love-lies-bleeding, swiss chard and beetroot	4 years
Legume	sweet peas, runner, French and broad beans, fenugreek	3–4 years
Onion	leeks, spring onions, ornamental Alliums	3 years
Tomato	all peppers, Chinese lanterns, petunias, *Salpiglossis*	3 years
Cucurbit	pumpkins, squashes, cucumbers, gourds	2–3 years
Daisy	lettuce, chicory, cornflowers, marigolds, chrysanthemums, cosmos, sunflowers	2–3 years
Grasses	sweetcorn, ornamental grasses	2–3 years
Labiate or Mint	*Agastache, Coleus, Nicotiana, Salvia,* lavender, bergamot, catmint	2 years
Carrot	carrots, coriander, dill, parsley, parsnips, fennel	1 year

so that the seed which comes from them will usually be similar or identical to the parent. Examples include peas and beans (but not sweet peas), sweet violets, tomatoes and peppers.

Seed saved from F1 plants, or from most variegated-leafed plants will not grow like the parent.

Most perennial flowers and species plants will come true to type, but growing your own seed from a small population will throw up occasional mutations, which may be of garden merit. Keep a sharp eye on the seedlings which germinate, checking for unusual leaf colours or growth forms. Breeders recommend growing an equal number of smaller, weaker seedlings as well as the robust ones, as these are often the choicest colours.

Seed, like all living things, keeps viable only for a limited time, and poor storage will age it rapidly. Ideally seed should be kept cool and dark at low humidity, but this isn't easy – some books recommend storing seeds in a biscuit tin in the bottom of your fridge, complete with a desiccant sachet or two, but this isn't really practical, especially if you grow a lot! The worst place to keep seed is in a hot, damp greenhouse with wildly fluctuating temperatures. For most people, and most seeds, somewhere with a constant temperature, just above frost-free, dry and dark is good enough. Keeping seeds in a cardboard box under the bed in an unheated spare room, or in a drawer in a cool, mouse-proof garage is a reasonable compromise.

REUSE, RETURN AND RECYCLE

Recycling should always be a feature of using materials sustainably in the garden, but some caution should be exercised as many plastics contain toxic residues which can poison plants. If you use food-grade plastic containers you should be safe. Computer and electrical equipment packaging is especially prone to exuding harmful chemicals, while certain metals should be avoided, particularly zinc, brass and copper. These are better weighed in for scrap than used to grow plants in, as the metal ions which leach out have toxic effects on plants grown in or close to them.

If new stone must be used for paved areas, use locally quarried material if it is available. If you select stone from abroad, go for firms which don't use child labour in their workforce.

Imagination is the key to recycling everything and anything. Just one example: use upturned beer or wine bottles, buried for three-quarters of their depth, to create a decorative edging to borders or paths which will show up in twilight with a soft reflected gleam.

In the greenhouse, well-washed yoghurt pots with holes punched in the base are fine for growing seedlings in. Pot them up into recycled ice-cream containers or opaque fruit punnets. For growing sweet peas, celeriac, runner beans or sweetcorn, you can make deeper, biodegradable containers from newspaper which disintegrate once planted out, thus minimizing root disturbance. Old toilet or kitchen paper roll inners are also excellent for plant growing, although they will need to be tightly packed, or tied up with string in their container to prevent them falling over.

In the coldframe using expanded polystyrene from mushroom or fish boxes for containers will provide insulation from cold earth and catch a little extra warmth to coddle your seedlings. The larger slotted plastic boxes used to supply mushrooms for shops are also deep enough to grow a crop of salads or other small plants such as short-rooted carrots, spring greens or even a mini-cauliflower or two.

On windowsills indoors utilize clear plastic fruit punnets, halved washed soft drink bottles or even a plastic bag held on a wire framework to act as mini-propagators over seedtrays made from vegetable or meat containers. Keep them watertight within a cat-litter tray or polystyrene tray, if you can find one narrow enough to fit on your windowsills.

Outside, old pop bottles with the base sawn off make marvellous mini-cloches to protect plants from cold and guard them against bird or slug damage. With care they will last at least two seasons.

Pots for Free

An industrial-sized mayonnaise or cooking oil drum makes a substantial pot which will take a tomato plant all the way to full-fruiting maturity, or a group of bulbs and a wallflower or two for spring display. If you want to cover the unsightly labels on a food container, use waterproof and weatherproof masonry or household paint, blackboard paint or acrylic-based multipurpose brush-on coating.

All containers with solid bases need to have drainage holes made in them. Use an electric drill to make a small initial hole and enlarge it using a craft knife, because this is much easier than trying to drill a huge hole. For a margarine tub holding around 1 gal (5 litres), you will need at least five holes of about ½in (1.5cm) diameter. To improve drainage, fill the first few inches with well-washed small pebbles, brick fragments or broken crockery, all of which serve just as well as the traditional broken flower-pot crocks.

Rigid plastic boxes intended for storing children's toys make handy sized planters for larger perennials, and old wooden drawers or kitchen cabinets can be stained, painted with a double layer of yacht varnish and planted up for immediate effect. Plastic mushroom crates will last for several seasons if kept shaded, as they degrade rapidly in full sun.

For bigger containers in prominent places, consider buying some of the ever-increasing range of bio-degradable pots. These won't disintegrate on the shelf and last for a couple of years in use, needing exposure to damp and sunlight to initiate breakdown. They look very much like high-quality terracotta, but are lighter in weight. They're especially appreciated if you're growing plants for a gift to a fellow gardener. Don't confuse these with the well-known blocks of compressed peat or coir which expand on being wetted and break down within weeks of being planted out directly into the soil. The biodegradable pot looks and is remarkably solid.

If you end up with masses of plastic pots which you won't use, either donate them to a local garden society – school garden clubs are always good homes for pots – or take them, even the broken ones, to a local garden centre or municipal tip for plastic recycling.

Railway sleepers are regularly recommended for garden building projects because they're relatively cheap and don't rot – but this is only because they've been pressure treated with creosote which will ooze out for years, damaging plant growth and ruining your clothes. Leave them to the people who spend their spare time rebuilding railways, and source old timber from buildings which are being demolished. A roof or flooring joist of

ABOVE: *Allotments are great places to discover inventive recycling.*

BELOW: *Bottle cloches protecting peas.*

softwood 4 × 4in (10 × 10cm) in thickness will take twenty years to decay (by then, you may well want to alter your design). Don't worry if there's a bit of woodworm; there are plenty of predators outside who eat woodboring grubs.

Use home-made potting mixtures to fill containers for perennials, bulbs and transplanting vegetables, saving commercial potting media for seed sowing.

Look After Your Bugs and Birds

Always try to incorporate a few native plants into your growing schemes. However studies have shown that to make a wildlife garden it doesn't need to be purely a copy of the natural landscape. A garden is an artificial space, however it is designed. From an insect point of view, the most important thing is to have as long a flowering season as possible, to provide pollen and nectar whenever there are creatures about. Once you have managed to build a vibrant microflora in your soil, a good insect population should follow, and birds will come freely of their own accord.

Broken bamboo canes cut into short lengths, tied up in bundles with wire and securely wedged in hedges or under the eaves of a shed create winter refuges for beneficial insects such lacewings, ladybirds and anthracoid bugs. Compost heaps, leaf heaps and log piles are other splendid hiding places, and areas which are not regularly disturbed are always helpful. Leave an area of long grass by a hedge uncut until early spring, to make a home for insects lodging in the base of the grasses or in the dead stems.

Growing plants for bird food is much cheaper than buying seed, and has the added advantage of being constantly available: if you go on holiday in the winter, can you always rely on the neighbours to feed your birds? Just for feeding birds is it ecologically sound to import peanuts or grains from poor countries whose inhabitants struggle to feed themselves? Suitable plants with plentiful berries include *Berberis* and *Sorbus spp*, *Sambucus* or *Malus*. Fruit growers will know that nothing attracts blackbirds like ripe redcurrants, so keep bushes netted if you want to enjoy the harvest yourself.

Remember that birds don't just eat berries, but seek out a variety of foods throughout the year: bluetits eat pollen and insects as well as suet. Take advantage of their habits by hanging fatballs up near roses or fruit bushes in winter, to encourage them to forage for hibernating insects, so removing pests. Leaving the last of the old flowerheads on plants until well into the winter will help – for example lavender seedheads are visited by sparrows and goldfinches. Bear in mind that while allowing birds to feed on what your garden can provide is always preferable to supplementary feeding, it's not always practical: you may want to eat brassicas yourself rather than feeding pigeons.

You can recycle for wildlife in the garden. Old enamel saucepans make perfect bird baths, and being heavy they don't tip up easily. For larger birds, sink an upturned dustbin lid into soft soil.

COMPOST
Peat and Other Mined Materials

The debate about peat use has raged among environmentalists and gardeners for decades, and the overwhelming consensus is that peat is not acceptable in the garden except for a few specialist areas.

Peat bogs take thousands of years to form the great depths which are being mined at present. They are valuable habitats for a range of specialist creatures and are carbon sinks. As peat is dug it releases buried carbon back into the atmosphere, contributing to global increases in carbon just as other fossil fuels do. In some parts of the world, peat is still used as a major fuel source, but in the UK it is principally used in horticulture. In 2000, nearly 3.5 million cubic metres of peat was used in Britain, with over 66 per cent used by amateur gardeners. Most of this originated from Ireland or Eastern Europe.

Peat came into favour because it was cheap, could be dug easily in vast quantity, was biologically inert, had minimal nutrient content but good water-holding capacity, a known pH, and could be milled easily to whatever grade of fineness was required. Manufacturers of commercial composts devoted over seventy years and a huge amount of money to producing and fine-tuning every conceivable compost which could be desired. Over the past twenty years various substitutes have been devised for peat, from coir (coconut fibre), bark shreds and sewage sludge to composted green waste. To date, none has been completely successful in superseding peat in all capacities, although many claim that this is only a matter of time and money. The logistics, to say nothing of the ethics, of shipping material such as coir, which could be used to improve soils, from countries with severe food shortages, have not yet been addressed.

Origanum vulgare with appreciative visitor.

ABOVE: *Mason bees work when conditions are too cold for hive bees, so encourage them to visit fruit trees by placing nest boxes like this one close to orchards.*

BELOW: *All sorts of insect home in on fallen timber for a refuge.*

Berberis wilsoniae *has prolific berries with spectacular autumn colour.*

Proprietary Compost

At present the most desirable proprietary compost mixtures from a horticultural standpoint are those which are free of pests or diseases, standardized as to particle size, nutrient levels and pH, have adequate drainage and water retaining capacity and are reasonably priced. On eco-friendly grounds you should add to these criteria those which have been produced closest to where you live from renewable materials such as bark, green or municipal waste, wool or other industrial by-products, in a manner which does not damage the environment.

For the home grower, the only possible use for peat is in specialist ericaceous composts or if growing in very small modules. Elsewhere there are a number of alternatives, and even the problems of ericaceous mixtures are gradually being overcome, with ingenious blends of composted bracken and sheep's wool. There is a small market in what is described as 'sustainable' peat, which is collected from the filters of hydro-electric power-stations.

Other ingredients of potting compost include some form of bulking agent to improve drainage, which is usually sharp sand, horticultural grit or a substitute such as vermiculite, a form of expanding mica. The best form of horticultural grit is granite. Sand, granite or vermiculite may be specifically mined or extracted as a by-product when seeking other minerals, but at present there is no way of knowing where the grit component of your compost comes from. There are some things that gardeners can control, and some that we can't, even with the best intentions.

Making Potting Compost

While proprietary peat-free potting compost is ideal for seed sowing, being sterile and with a measured quantity of nutrients, for established container plants it's much better for the planet if you can reduce the need to ship bulky ingredients countrywide by making your own compost.

Loam is a favourite ingredient, but it's not

always easy to produce in a crowded or newly made garden. If you have cleared an area of lawn to enlarge a bed or new plantings, make it into a loam stack by putting the turves upside down, covering with black plastic and leaving for a year before use. Then chop the decayed turf well with a spade – or sieve it if you're fussy about ideal texture, using a 1/2in (1cm) diameter sieve – before adding it to a potting compost mixture. An alternative source of loam is molehill tops, which are free of pests and often finer textured than the surrounding soil. Removing the tops will not hurt the mole, provided you leave the run covered.

Spent Compost

When the plants growing in the potting compost are renewed or moved to bigger pots, all spent

Salad collection growing in home-made potting compost.

compost, provided it comes from healthy plants, should be returned to bare soil to improve the texture. Plants which have died from a root-based disease such as wilt, or pests like vine weevil shouldn't have their pot contents placed directly on the soil. Instead spread it out on plastic sheeting to expose it to the sun and air for several days before composting it, or sending it to the local tip as green waste where it can be composted at high temperatures and rendered safe.

CHAPTER 3

Water

SAVING WATER

Rainwater is best for your plants – it's what they're designed to drink. Unlike tap water, rain doesn't contain chlorine, fluoride, aluminium and other additives which might be present in tap water – and it's free. Using highly purified tap water for plants is both wasteful and ecologically unsustainable. The energy and effort involved in producing drinking water is immense, making it a precious scarce resource which should be saved for its original purpose, drinking or cooking.

The biggest problem for rainwater is how and where to store it. Even in the dry south-eastern areas of the UK, a small roof can shed up to 100,000 litres annually! Most gardens will already have a waterbutt, but if you haven't then it's one of the items of equipment you really ought to go out and buy.

As well as the main house, every garden building should have some method of water collection, and large plots should have a selection of water storage points throughout the garden. If you have shorter distances to walk carrying a watering can, you'll be more likely to use one, rather than reaching for the hosepipe. Ideally these storage points should all be supplied with rainwater rather than mains, although this is not always easy unless you have a pump, or garden on a slope. When siting a waterbutt, always make sure the stand is secure, as the weight of the contents changes, but that it is also high enough off the ground to place the largest watering can you have underneath. Keep out mosquitoes and inquisitive pets or children, by fitting butts with close-fitting, opaque covers; and if fed from a gutter near shrubs or trees, put a scrunched-up ball of wire netting in the entrance

to the downpipe, to trap leaves. This will need regular checking and cleaning, or the gutter will overflow.

A single waterbutt will hold at most 50–55 gal (210–239 litres), which will serve to soak a moderate collection of pots for perhaps ten days in very hot weather, when container plants will demand watering at least twice a day. Doubling up waterbutts is a useful practice, and you can install as many as you have room for, but not many gardens have space to collect as much as they will need during a hot summer. Several manufacturers are

Collecting rainwater has been vital for centuries: this example dates from the late 1770s.

Frog and spawn.

Everything can be recycled, especially if it's watertight.

Rainwater collected from the local chapel roof feeds watertanks made from recycled cattle feed containers for the allotment holders at Groby, Leicestershire.

now making thinner, taller waterbutts to accommodate awkward sites, so it's well worth checking out these different options, although unfortunately unconventional shapes are often more costly.

If you want to make your own waterbutts, look for containers which have been used to store fruit juices or other industrial scale food products, as they will be safe to re-use. For the larger garden, it's always worth looking at bigger alternative water containers. Household water tanks are usually fairly cheap, although older models will eventually rust, being made of galvanized steel. Large plastic tanks which have been used in cattle-feed or milk production are sometimes offered second-hand at farm sales, and these can be extremely good value for money if not always very attractive to look at. If you're fitting a tank above ground, it may be possible to site it uphill for gravity to feed water where it's needed.

In an ideal situation, as much of the rainwater as possible falling on the roof would be collected in an underground tank, then pumped to feed a series of hosepipes. Underground storage schemes are not cheap, especially if fitted long after the house was built. As an investment, they will make a worthwhile addition to the value of a property and should last for over fifty years if installed properly. If you collect all the storm water which runs off from your house and garden you will be entitled to a permanent reduction in water rates.

Before thinking of any type of major underground work, consult your local authority to find out what regulations are in place, as you may need planning permission. It's also a good idea to ring your local cable information hotline service providers to determine if there is likely to be a known underground connection near where you're excavating. In the UK BT cableline is a free service for anybody digging holes. If you cut a cable and haven't rung the number then BT will charge you for the cost of reconnecting it – but if you ring them first but still accidentally cut something, there is no fee. The current number (Sept 2008) is 0800 917 3993.

IRRIGATION AND WATER USE

The best way to water your garden, say the water companies, is by not needing to. Grow drought-resistant plants, use water-retentive mulches and

Euphorbias are good drought-resistant subjects for sunny, poor draining soils.

ABOVE: *Silver- and grey-leaved foliage usually indicates a plant adapted to dry conditions: here they are growing in a shallow limestone soil barely 6in/15cm deep.*

BELOW: *Watering cans at the ready.*

add plenty of organic matter to your soil to produce a humus rich, moisture retaining soil. Sadly, the British weather rarely co-operates for longer than a few weeks, and conditions rarely remain constant. UK gardeners often suffer alternate droughts or sudden deluges, and drought-loving plants don't cope well with winter waterlogging. The more likely solution is to site drought lovers carefully, in the highest spots, and put tough subjects which can cope with floods or dry spells elsewhere.

On a small scale, watering cans are the most economical method of irrigation, but their use tends to be self-limiting after a number of trips, because of the effort involved. A 2-gallon watering can weighs at least 20lb (10kg), so a session with your potted plants can be just as healthy a workout for your muscle and cardiovascular development as a trip to the gym.

Watering cans are ideal for irrigating small areas of pots, young seedlings or one or two newly transplanted trees. For larger areas or if you plan to be away frequently during the summer, consider using micro-irrigation, with either many small-bore pipes feeding individual pots, or a porous pipe to deliver water to a specific area of garden.

Micro-irrigation can be set up to automatically deliver water at set times, using a clock setting similar to that on a central heating system, or for the more sophisticated by measuring the soil moisture in a given site and irrigating when a particular level of dryness is reached. If you are lucky enough to have a greenhouse, a solar-powered pump can also be activated to provide irrigation after a certain number of hours of sunlight. Micro-irrigation is a very efficient use of water, because it delivers only to the areas where it is needed, and as pipes are at low pressure leaks are minimal. Unfortunately at the time of writing the water companies treat these systems as being exactly the same as a sprinkler, which is much more extravagant, and they demand additional charges if the water comes directly from the mains supply.

Using rainwater instead of mains water for micro-irrigation is not only cheaper but can prolong the life of your equipment as it doesn't contain dissolved calcium salts which can precipitate out to clog up the pipes.

Gardeners on a slope can use gravity to their advantage, especially during water restrictions if they have access to old guttering or lengths of drainpipe, and many allotment holders devise ingenious methods of irrigation, even during a hosepipe ban, to water their precious seedlings.

WHAT SHOULD I WATER?

Many plants only need extra water at certain stages of their development, and a little drought-stress can actually improve their performance – for example, many silver leaved subjects will only shine if they have hot dry conditions. For maximum benefit, irrigate in the cool of the evening when the plants have the longest time to take up liquids. If you have only limited time or limited water, select the most water-demanding subjects to make the most of your resources.

As a rule, most perennial plants only need

Watering by sprinkler is wasteful of water.

watering when newly established, or if about to flower in extremely dry spells. Watering will prolong flower life, and encourage further flowerbud formation, but most plants can cope with short-lived drought conditions, although fruiting and flowering may be diminished or pest and disease attack aggravated. They may wilt at mid-day but should revive after cool dawn dew, and only if you notice them failing to perk up in the morning should you irrigate in late evening.

Vegetables are assumed to be heavy water users, but not all are equally demanding: potatoes, onions, peas and beans are most rewarding if watered at specific times. Some plants such as beetroot will go to seed (bolt) rapidly if deprived of water at critical periods. Water potatoes when tubers are just about to form, peas and beans as the flowers are starting to set, and onions when the bulbs are beginning to swell. Watering tomatoes and squashes growing in open ground in dry periods will make them grow large but not necessarily more flavoursome: small fruits are more concentrated in taste. Members of the cucurbit group often produce male, not female, flowers when subject to heat or other stress, so fruits aren't produced. To overcome this without heavy watering, snap off the male flowers (they're the ones without a little bump behind the petals) and use in various delicious recipes, so encouraging female flower production.

Dahlias are deep-rooted but fleshy-leaved, and need regular watering in dry spells to look their best.

Established fruit bushes and trees rarely need irrigation, the exceptions being cherries in late May when insufficient water will cause fruit drop, or raspberries in long hot summers when fruits dry up and shrivel on unwatered plants.

If sowing seeds in dry soil, make a deeper drill than normal and water it until the soil is well-soaked (puddled) before scattering seed. This should last until the seeds begin to germinate, when additional watering may be required if the weather conditions remain the same. Many annuals such as sweet peas and dahlias will perform better if well-watered during hot conditions. To improve water retention, apply a thin 1–2in (2–4cm) layer of lawn mowings to damp soil around the roots of the plants, and replenish every time you mow the lawn.

Container plants are not always sustainable or desirable in an ecologically sound garden: they will always require additional water and feeding, and so cannot be self-supporting. Pots need much more care than those growing in open ground, but for those with limited space or difficult areas such as roof gardens, container plants can be the only method of growing.

Try to use permanent containers such as pots rather than disposable growbags wherever appropriate, and make your own growing media, using garden compost, leafmould and loam mixed with grit, vermiculite or composted bark. Always select the largest possible container that will have a reserve of waterholding capacity for established plants such as tender fruit trees. Water well and infrequently rather than little and often, always in

the coolest part of the evening where plants have the whole night to adsorb liquid, rather than in the heat of the day. Don't spray water around unless you have thoroughly wetted the base of plants, as high air humidity and dry roots are a sure recipe for powdery mildew.

The proprietary gels and wetting agents sold to improve water retention in composts work to a limited extent in summer, although when over-dry they lock up water that plant roots cannot access easily. Using them is dangerous in winter when they prevent excess liquid from draining, aggravating frost damage to both plants and pots.

Sometimes containers are the only possible method of growing.

COPING WITH EXTREMES

Excessive rainfall can be just as damaging to the garden as too little (and much more depressing to the gardener). Problems exacerbated by high water levels include plants dying by drowning when water fills all the gaps in the soil pores, which destroys aerobic soil life, leading to foul-smelling root rots as everything growing in the soil decays. Slugs and snails go into overdrive reproduction, fungal diseases abound and nutrients are washed away by heavy rain, polluting land downstream. Flower and fruit production can be minimal if heavy rain is prolonged, while shoots and leaves

Snails and slugs are among the most common garden foes.

grow rapidly with soft, sappy shoots which attract pest attack.

Long-lived drought is probably less common in the UK than too much water. Permanent wilting point is the stage at which plants fail to respond even after a soaking, and some damage is inevitable at this point, although most will recover after a growth check. Trees and shrubs will shed leaves if subjected to severe water stress, but this doesn't necessarily mean they are dying: it's a self-defence mechanism to conserve water, and they will revive once it rains.

Don't dig in very dry conditions, as it exposes

Some plants like these hostas will tolerate high rainfall, but watch out for slugs.

a larger soil surface to the air which dries out quicker. Hoeing to remove even seedling weeds is beneficial, but the old gardener's advice about creating a 'dust mulch' to keep plants moist is misfounded – the hoe's benefit comes solely from reducing weed competition.

Mulching damp soil retains moisture and slows down runoff as well as keeping plant roots cooler in summer. During winter heavy mulches (particularly light-coloured ones such as straw) can insulate the ground very thoroughly and prevent it releasing warmth on cold nights, when the soil is warmer than the surrounding air. To avoid frost damage, choose a dark-coloured mulch or in late autumn rake back material immediately under plants which open their blooms early, such as *Viburnum x bodnatense,* blackcurrant bushes or camellias. Mulches to improve water retention can include short-lived materials such as newspaper with straw or bark spread on top to weigh it down, which is useful around trees and fruit bushes, or longer-lived chipped bark, shredded hedge clippings and municipal compost.

Inserting perforated plastic pipe deeply into large pots as you plant them up will make sure that when these are filled, water goes direct to the roots instead of pooling on the surface and running down pot sides without wetting the compost. Aim water onto the soil surface, not onto the leaves. Site pots appropriately, in areas which will be shaded during the hottest parts of the day.

USING GREY WATER

'Grey' water is the rather unlovely name for once-used water, like that from a bath or washing-up which is normally flushed down the drains. Depending on what it's been used for, it may contain high levels of potash, principally derived from soaps and detergents. These aren't usually a problem if grey water's occasionally used on the garden (the potassium salts can act as a plant food), but if applied regularly or in very hot conditions it can cause scorching of tender young foliage. High levels of detergent can also strip protective layers from leaf surfaces and damage microbial populations in the soil.

If you want to reuse grey water, avoid the discharge from dishwashers which is unsuitable for irrigation. Waste water from washing machines is better employed as an occasional emergency top up for the garden, with the main use restricted to flushing the lavatory. Water from a shower or bath where only soap is used is fine, but should be freshly collected, as the build up of fats and oils from spent skin cells quickly becomes smelly, as well as causing grease deposits which block piping. Loose hair from bathwater can also be a problem, collecting debris and looking unpleasant.

You should rotate grey water around the garden, to avoid build-up of potentially dangerous chemicals. Acid loving plants such as blueberries or azaleas don't like grey water, and because of the danger of contamination from skin-living bacteria, don't use it for salad plants either.

From an upstairs bathroom there are a number of small handheld or battery powered devices which can be used to siphon bathwater to a water-butt outside or directly to a hosepipe. Some of these are now being made with solar powered chargers. Downstairs, have a bucket handy beside the kitchen sink, where you can pour off surplus liquid, such as water which has been used for boiling potatoes or other vegetables, or the cold water run off waiting for the hot to come through the pipes, for example – and transfer it to a watering can when you next go outside.

RAINGARDENS AND RUNOFF

In natural situations, very little of the water falling on an area of trees or grassland runs away. Most is either taken up by plant roots, evaporates or seeps slowly through the soil to replenish groundwater. Once land has been built on in towns and cities with almost total covering of the soil surfaces with impermeable tarmac or paving and a massively increased surface area from the roofs of buildings which are designed to shed water quickly, the situation is dramatically reversed, with almost all of the water running off and very little sinking through to feed underground reserves.

During times of sudden heavy rain most of the rain which falls on our gardens is fed via

Where drainage is slow and rainfall high, plants such as this fairy foxglove, Erinus alpinus, *thrive. Here they will reduce rapid rainwater runoff and help prevent flash flooding.*

stormdrains to sewers, which often overflow if filled too rapidly, especially if a number of new houses have been built since the initial drainage system was dug. When existing sewers are unable to cope with the excessive flow of storm water it can cause, at the worst, flooding of houses or at very least, unpleasant smells and risk of disease.

Causes of rapid runoff include the paving over of front gardens to create car-parking, and increased popularity of hard landscaping such as patios, decking or other non-porous garden features. If you need to park your car off the road, try to devote as much of the area as possible to planted space. A newly introduced planning requirement means that anyone wanting to cover over 6 sq yd/m of front garden will need planning permission if they use a non-permeable product.

A method of slowing down the flow of runoff to the advantage of both you and the rest of the neighbourhood is called raingardening, which involves planting areas of water-retentive vegetation to maximize the saving of whatever water falls on your plot for as long a time as possible. Raingardening claims to help reduce water bills by demand for individual garden irrigation, reducing need for stormwater provision and increasing flow to natural aquifers. An idea which originally came

Meadowsweet is a native indicator plant for damp sites.

WHAT COUNTS AS PERMEABLE PAVING?

Hard landscaping which allows rainwater to trickle through slowly, rather than run off rapidly, is termed permeable.

Permeable materials include:

- Permanent aggregates such as mill-waste, slate chippings, recycled plastic or rubber crumbs, glass cullet; in very dry climates these can encourage dew to form overnight, so creating a very small water source for the plants
- Self bonding aggregate (sometimes known as hoggin)
- Turf reinforcements (usually rubber, plastic or concrete grids, sections or interlocking slabs)
- Slabs with large gaps between or laid alternately, to allow planting between them
- Porous block paving, which can be perforated or have a fairly loose-textured finish, similar to breeze blocks; sometimes manufactured from recycled material, such as plastic or rubber

Permeable asphalt is not recommended, unless already in place, as it is difficult to keep weed free and can contribute to pollution.

And remember, you can always use a semi-permanent biodegradable mulch such as chipped bark, laid over reinforced plastic mesh for long-lived pedestrian use.

---

from the dry Midwestern states of America, this won't be needed in all parts of the UK, but may well prove attractive in the drier South East.

Raingardens are either artificially dug hollows or naturally occurring damp spots which are filled with native plants tolerant of occasional soakings, heavily mulched with large bark chips or coarse pebbles. They should be sited a safe distance from buildings, at least 10ft (3m) away from a house wall, and fed from gutters or other runoff sources. Ideally make a raingarden in a sunny spot, to encourage rapid evaporation of collected water and avoid breeding mosquitoes.

The design of a raingarden would mimic the most naturally water adsorbing planting – deciduous trees in summer, leafy perennials and long grass – and incorporate these features in low-lying areas of the garden, such as sinuous trails of grasses growing in shallow furrows threading through a flowerbed, leading downwards to a sunken area

of moisture loving perennials such as candelabra primroses, *Rogersias* and ferns. For a more minimalist design rainwater could be directed along flow-form gutters lined with brilliantly coloured recycled glass, to settle in a downward spiral of pebbles which tops a soakaway, perhaps with a clump of twisted rush as a centrepiece.

Rapid runoff can lead to problems elsewhere in the garden too, by causing pollution, even from unexpected sources. Small garden buildings, such as sheds, are often topped with a covering of roofing felt, which releases harmful petroleum-based chemicals. Green roofing eliminates the problem, releasing rainwater slowly to a waterbutt or pond after purifying it through passing between the pebbles and living roots.

Manure and garden compost should be only dug in during the growing season, or about six weeks before the season starts, as excess nitrogen is leached out through the soil in winter rain, contributing to pollution of streams and rivers.

REEDBEDS

For those with a very large garden, or having a sizeable area of hard surfacing to drain, a reedbed offers simple natural water purification, particularly if the water has been contaminated with organic matter such as grey water, sewage outfall or manure-contaminated runoff before releasing water back to rivers and streams. Sadly, most gardeners will only be able to dream of such schemes, although they're being installed in new housing developments, and reedbeds with adjoining ponds are becoming a common sight by new business parks, motorways or shopping malls.

There is an increasing recognition of the benefits of the micro-organisms which live on the massive root system of the common reed (*Phragmites communis*) which are able to filter and remove toxins from the water in which the reeds are growing. Reeds have hollow stems which transport oxygen down to the roots, unlike many other water plants, and this helps the bacteria break down organic chemicals quicker.

Reedbeds are used successfully to treat sewage from small businesses, allotment groups or individual households sited away from mains supplies: they're a useful and much more decorative alternative to a septic tank, needing low maintenance and costing little to run once installed.

Reeds are very invasive, however, and should be rigorously contained on a garden scale. There are two types of reedbed, horizontal and vertical. Vertical ones are more efficient and take up less room. In both types, reeds are planted on a layer of coarse gravel, with a smaller layer of pea gravel on top, and spaced about 2ft (60cm) apart. To keep the reeds healthy, cut them down to water level in autumn when the leaves can be composted: the reedbed will need resting after this to recover. You need a reedbed area of up to 3 sq yd/m per person in a household for complete grey water purification, and in temperate regions such as the UK this will only be useable for the warmer seasons of the year.

For more information, especially about using reedbeds for sewage treatment, visit the Centre for Alternative Technology or the Rodale Foundation websites.

PONDS

Ponds are a must-have feature in the garden, being the equivalent of an en-suite bath, bedroom and diner for the local wildlife. They provide a focal point and a natural gathering place. Sadly, many gardeners decide that they should fill in their ponds as soon as they have children, fearing death by drowning.

It is possible to have small children and a pond! Like many other aspects of parenthood, it needs a bit of ingenuity and rearrangement of the garden. There are several methods of child-proofing water features. Probably the easiest method is to have a shallow pebble-lined bed with a single small fountain or bubble jet, perhaps flowing over rocks, which will enable birds and insects to still drink but will be too shallow for a child to drown in. These can be dug into the ground or raised on a shallow platform, with the mechanics hidden behind planks or slabs. When building this type of feature, be sure to check every pebble used for the display in case it has rough edges which might pierce the butyl lining. It's often helpful to install a soakaway to cope with heavy rainfall raising the water level. This can be very simple in design – just extending the pebbled area beyond the butyl liner will assist drainage, and you only need attractive stones on the top.

Wall-mounted basins can be set high above the children's heads or can be selected deliberately to be too narrow for a child to access – these make a feature from an otherwise dull area of brickwork and are very effective in town terraced gardens, where the sound of moving water helps blur out unwelcome background noise.

Another method of keeping water in the garden is to plant up water-filled containers (or to

A bridge over even a small pond encourages people to look down and observe wildlife.

A solar powered flow-form helps oxygenate water.

Flowering rush Butomus umbellatus, *a beautiful UK native which inhabits shallow water at pond margins.*

waterproof existing pots by filling in drainage holes using bathroom sealant and painting the sides with yacht varnish), using striking marginal pond plants such as flowering rush or bur-reed. There will still be enough water around the pot edges for insects to drink from, but insufficient to be dangerous for small inquisitive humans. If you have a smooth-sided raised trough or barrel with the edge at least 3ft/1m above ground level, it's difficult for toddlers to climb into, and anything over 2ft (60cm) diameter will be too heavy for them to pull over once filled with water as well as plants.

If you want to enjoy watching frogs with your kids, you'll need a full-sized pool at least 12in (30cm) deep, and even deeper if the amphibians are to overwinter, so consider a pond-cover. A cover can be the most expensive option but are probably the most successful method of separating water and young children – the cover will protect pond creatures from predators and can be used as a garden feature long after your children have grown up. You can choose from a sturdy metal grid which sits just below the surface of the water and appears invisible from even a short distance, or an above-ground frame which bolts together and can be dismantled for periodic pond maintenance.

Making a Pond

Ponds are now almost always lined with butyl, thick rubber sheeting, the best quality having a lifespan of around thirty years. Butyl has some problems, including the initial cost, the necessity of concealing the edges and difficulty of repairing leaks if accidentally punctured. A pond lined with butyl should be dug out considerably deeper than the initial depth of water required, to allow for a deep layer of sand covering the area the pond will take, so avoiding danger of stones rising in the soil to perforate the rubber. To avoid steep curves or sharp edges which can stress the rubber, only use gentle slopes in the design, tuck in all folds well underneath and try to keep all edges above ground shaded with stones when planting. Butyl will deteriorate in sunlight so edges above ground should be covered and ponds kept topped up whenever levels drop.

Pondcovers can be decorative…

…or purely functional.

Goldfish can be compatible with frogs, provided there is plenty of cover for tadpoles and young frogs to hide in.

PLANTS FOR POND MARGINS, RAINGARDENS AND WET SPOTS

The following species should be quite happy to have wet feet from time to time, but survive equally well in drier conditions.

Larger Shrubs and Small Trees

Aronia melanocarpa
Betula especially *B. nigra, B. papyrifera, B. populifolia, B. pubescens*
Clethra alnifolia
Cornus controversa, C. florida, C. stolonifera 'Kelsayii'
Kalmia (all)
Salix – especially the slightly less vigorous forms such as *S. daphnoides, S. eleagnoides, S. melanostachys*
Viburnum opulis, V. plicatum

Herbaceous Plants

Acorus calmus
Angelica – particularly the spectacularly coloured *A. gigas* or *A. sylvestris 'Purpurea'*

Artemisia 'Guizho group'	*Lythrum salicaria*
Eupatorium spp	*Monarda didyma*
Echinacea purpurea	*Primula japonica*
Iris kaempferi, I. siberica	*Verbena hastata*

Before the advent of butyl, ponds were sometimes made from preformed concrete or plastic sections, some of which are still around today. Such ponds are easy to excavate and less susceptible to perforation than butyl but come in a limited choice of design and size. They can also look very artificial. Plastic pond linings sometimes contain potentially carcinogenic additives, and can release chlorine into the environment as they degrade.

The Romans used hydraulic cement to line their aqueducts, baths and water gardens, and a similar material, Portland cement, is still around today. It's very longlasting. Probably the ideal earth-friendly choice is to line the pond with puddle clay, or bentonite laid onto a membrane. This is a very long-lasting natural material, with a lifespan of over a hundred years. It's capable of being laid in much more challenging shapes than butyl, coping with frequent changes of direction and avoiding the need to tuck edges under on corners. Puddleclay is available in roll form but is heavy, expensive and needs experience to lay it exactly. There aren't many suppliers either! Like butyl it deteriorates if allowed to dry out completely, but can be repaired, although it's not easy.

In heavy clay soils, a low-lying patch in the garden can be dug out and allowed to fill naturally, and will remain wet during most of the year. Clay is capable of retaining as much as 60 per cent of the water which falls on it, so you might as well turn this to your advantage with a permanent damp-loving planting, rather than trying to drain or regularly cultivate such a soggy soil.

You should never use fresh mains water to top up a garden pond, as the chemicals used to make our water fit to drink make it equally toxic to water creatures, so if at all possible use rainwater – if you can't, fill an empty waterbutt from the tap using a hosepipe and wait 24 hours, when the chlorine will have evaporated, before transferring it to the pond.

Most textbooks state that to help amphibians, your pond shouldn't contain goldfish too, but provided there are areas with shallow water where adult fish can't reach easily, and plenty of aquatic plants for cover, frogs and fish seem to be able to coexist. To encourage frogs and newts to over-winter successfully, either leave plenty of dry leaves under hedgerows or make a special hybernaculum, by piling up old bricks or logs and covering it with turf. They'll repay your hard work by eating slugs and snails throughout the growing season.

Hedgehogs are as suicidal as lemmings for having a self-destructive urge: if there is any way at all of getting stuck or falling into something, a hedgehog will find it. Make sure your pond has a sloping edge so any short-sighted hedgehog who takes a stroll off the bank and ends up swimming can climb out.

There are plenty of books giving extensive advice about planting and stocking ponds which applies to any garden, not just ecologically aware ones. Select a variety of native species, as well as others, and incorporate a mixture of aquatic, surface and marginal plants. Use common sense: don't place the pond in deep shade or under a big tree, and have a range of depths to suit both animals and plants.

CHAPTER 4

Composting

Everybody can – and should – make compost. A good compost heap is the powerhouse of your garden.

Anything which was alive once will naturally decay, and composting is merely a way of allowing this to happen with minimum loss of plant nutrients in a convenient place. Really good crumbly compost should look like an excellent fruit cake: a well blended dark, rich and inviting mixture of indistinguishable ingredients.

Adding compost to your soil improves the health of the soil microflora, which in turn leads to healthier plants. Forensic scientists can identify an individual area by its soil microflora, so in a sense every garden has its own fingerprint, which can be improved and increased by the care of the gardener.

Micro-organisms in the soil interlink with plant roots in various forms, known as mycorrhiza, which can be a coating on the outside of the root, in specialized areas within roots, as in the nodules on legumes which fix nitrogen, or merely an association of particular organisms with certain groups of plants. This symbiotic relationship was first observed in trees, but is now known to be present in almost all growing plants, although the most established and complex relationships are with long-lived subjects. Such intimate relationships mean that the plant benefits from a vastly increased root area, so minerals are more easily adsorbed. Some soil organisms produce protective antibiotic-like effects, which defend plants against disease or predators.

Regular use of compost will gradually build up humus levels in the soil, improving its water-retaining capacity, texture and make a wider range of nutrients available to plants growing in it.

Compost ingredients.

MAKING GARDEN COMPOST

To make compost, you need equal parts of green and brown wastes, a sheltered corner of your garden and time.

Put a layer of twiggy prunings on the bottom of the area where you will make your heap, and stack the material in layers about 4–6in (10–15cm) thick of alternate green and brown waste. Cover with an old carpet, cardboard or layer of hardboard to keep the warmth in and excess rainwater out.

Leaves can be added to the compost heap or made into leafmould.

After you have made a heap, keep topping it up for several months, until it stops sinking dramatically in height a few days after filling.

If the heap is becoming wet and smelly, add more twiggy pieces or scrunched-up newspaper, toilet roll inners or crumpled cardboard, such as egg boxes. In very dry weather or in strong winds the heap may need watering to keep it moist.

Leave the heap for at least four to six months, depending on the time of year. To examine it, first remove the initial top layer, which may not have completely broken down. If the compost is dark in colour with bright red or striped worms present, leave it for another month, but if there are plenty of woodlice and spiders visible, it's ready to use.

'Hot compost' is made by stacking a large amount of mixed material in a large heap quickly – ideally in a single day. The heap can reach very high temperatures – easily 75°C – in the centre, which kill off any weed seeds or disease spores (as in an overheated haystack, although unlike hay, compost doesn't catch fire). To accelerate the turnover of a hot compost heap, dismantle the heap and restack it as it's cooled down and sunk a little.

'Cold compost' is made by adding small amounts of material over a long time to make a heap. This method produces perfectly acceptable compost but won't kill as many weed seeds.

Human urine has long been a traditional addition to the compost heap. It is not essential, but does contain appreciable amounts of nitrogen and trace elements, as well as accelerating bacterial fermentation processes. Urine-containing composts shouldn't be used on salad crops, or other produce which is eaten raw, to reduce any risk of disease. For those of a hardy disposition, urine diluted with equal parts of water can be a useful nitrogenous feed for container plants.

Woody material which is too thick to break down can be left stacked in a heap, where it will decompose slowly over several years during which time it may become a useful wildlife habitat, or it can be shredded. The most efficient shredders are petrol driven rather than electric. It may be helpful to share the cost of hiring occasionally with neighbours rather than buying one. Avoid having bonfires if possible – they're antisocial in urban

Green chipping waste from a contractor needs thorough composting before use to reduce any danger of disease transmission.

areas, and the smoke contains high levels of carcinogens.

Garden compost is relatively rich in nutrients, containing up to 5 per cent potassium, with lower levels of nitrogen and phosphorus, but its real value is a source of humus and beneficial microbes. Compost can be applied as a mulch or dug in as required, but avoid applying heavy mulches of compost in early autumn, when minerals will be leached away over the winter, unless you plan to plant or sow a crop within the next six weeks. Organic gardeners are recommended to use not more than two full wheelbarrows of compost per 5 sq yd/m per year, although this can be varied according to the soil conditions and intensity of cropping.

Compost shouldn't be used on the areas you plan to grow root vegetables for the growing season, as carrots and parsnips often develop

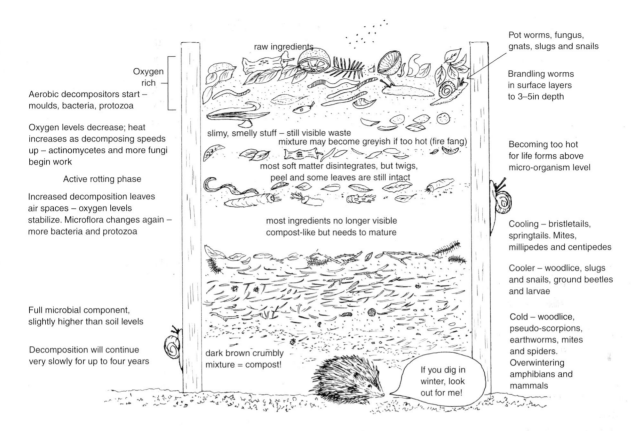

raw ingredients

Pot worms, fungus, gnats, slugs and snails

Brandling worms in surface layers to 3–5in depth

Oxygen rich

Aerobic decompositors start – moulds, bacteria, protozoa

Oxygen levels decrease; heat increases as decomposing speeds up – actinomycetes and more fungi begin work

Active rotting phase

Increased decomposition leaves air spaces – oxygen levels stabilize. Microflora changes again – more bacteria and protozoa

slimy, smelly stuff – still visible waste
mixture may become greyish if too hot (fire fang)

most soft matter disintegrates, but twigs, peel and some leaves are still intact

most ingredients no longer visible compost-like but needs to mature

Becoming too hot for life forms above micro-organism level

Cooling – bristletails, springtails. Mites, millipedes and centipedes

Cooler – woodlice, slugs and snails, ground beetles and larvae

Full microbial component, slightly higher than soil levels

Decomposition will continue very slowly for up to four years

dark brown crumbly mixture = compost!

If you dig in winter, look out for me!

Cold – woodlice, pseudo-scorpions, earthworms, mites and spiders. Overwintering amphibians and mammals

What happens in a compost heap.

forked roots after heavy dressings of compost immediately before sowing.

Garden compost can contain weed seeds which are still viable (or other unwelcome ingredients such as slug eggs) especially when made slowly, so is not suitable for potting compost except for use in established container plants, unless you are confident of identifying weed seedlings as they emerge.

COMPOST TEA

The use of compost tea is an exciting but relatively new development in horticulture. For many years organic gardeners had been soaking fresh leafy material (such as nettles, comfrey or seaweed) in water until it rotted, then feeding the liquid to their plants. This practice had a far greater effect on the plants than would have been justified by nutrient quantity in the liquid alone, and it was suggested that the observed improvement in growth was caused by an increase in the number of beneficial micro-organisms.

After research it was concluded that best results came from aerobic microbes, which had greater influence on plant roots. These are commercially cultured by rapid oxygen-rich fermentation in controlled conditions, producing a highly concentrated liquid extract which is then diluted before being applied to plants.

Compost tea is claimed to have great benefits in promoting increased rooting, flowering and fruiting, as well as generally improving plant health. A number of commercial nurseries in the UK and Europe have taken up the method. Stabilized compost tea concentrates are now available to the public. They keep for six months or more if undiluted and should be used in the concentrations recommended on the label.

WHAT COMPOSTER?

If you leave vegetation lying in a heap it will rot down, but a container for compost looks tidier and can encourage faster decomposition. You will need at least two containers, one for filling while the other one matures. A container should be strong, with a wide area for filling, and easy to empty. Make sure you have allowed room for wheelbarrow access and space to swing a garden fork.

A compost heap doesn't have to stand on bare soil in order to work, provided you add a spadeful of soil, or better still a spadeful of already composted material, to the lower layers to start it off (like yeast in bread, this will prime the heap with the correct bacteria.) Slabs or a semi-permeable membrane are easier to shovel the matured compost from once your heap has finished working.

The plastic Dalek type cone bins given away or sold cheaply by many local councils are not ideal, often being insufficiently ventilated, encouraging the contents to become anaerobic and over-wet, leading to a putrefied foul-smelling mess. To avoid

A collection of composters on display at Ryton Organic Gardens.

this problem add extra brown waste (*see* page 51) which is high in carbon and provides air spaces, ensuring good drainage and better air circulation.

Cone bins are ideal for closed compost methods for perennial weed disposal, but will need to be placed on a hard surface with no cracks which weeds may regenerate from. (For really tough weeds such as couch grass, secure the compost bin to the slab by slathering a generous layer of bathroom sealant around the base of the bin a day before you start to fill it; this prevents any roots making their escape.) Cone bins are quickly filled, especially if you have a medium to large lawn, and access to the mature compost is often very awkward. At least two bins are required by a garden of only 20 sq yd/m.

For bigger gardens two or more larger-capacity bins are less labour-intensive than a multitude of smaller ones. A good type of bigger bin is the square or oblong one, made in unfolding or clip-together sections from recycled plastic. Like the cone bins, you can often buy them at a reduced price from local authorities.

An attractive large compost container made from wood is the 'New Zealand' design, which has removable slats to get at the compost easily. This type of bin can be homemade if you have basic carpentry skills. Wood based compost containers

---

COMPOST CONTAINERS

A glance at any garden catalogue will show a huge variety of compost container designs. Should you feel tempted to buy one, ask yourself the following:

- How much garden and kitchen waste am I likely to produce?
  If you are only just starting to grow your own vegetables you may be surprised at how much peeling and other waste is generated. As a guide, a 10 × 60ft (3 × 20m) garden used for intensive vegetable and fruit growing, with all the produce used in the kitchen, will need to compost around 0.75 cu yd/m of waste every six to nine months.
- How easy is it going to be to dig out the finished compost?
  You should be able to remove an entire side or dismantle the box in sections without difficulty.
- How sturdy is the container, and is there any method of securing it?
- Compost can be very heavy, especially when wet, and if you're regularly manoeuvring a wheelbarrow round a structure it needs to be able to withstand occasional knocks and bangs. Empty plastic bins can easily blow over on a windy site, and in some areas foxes or badgers seeking for worms become a pest.

GREEN AND BROWN WASTES FOR YOUR COMPOST HEAP

'**Green**' materials are soft and sappy, rot quickly and often contain higher levels of nitrogen.

Add:
Non-seeding annual weeds
Leaves only from perennial weeds which don't prop-agate from stem cuttings, e.g. dandelion, young nettles, docks
Comfrey leaves
Vegetable and fruit cores, peelings and husks
Lawnmowings
Healthy dead flowers, leaves and other garden waste, e.g. pea, bean, potato or tomato haulms (stems), old herbaceous stems, discarded pot plants
Herbivorous animal manures and cage cleanings, e.g. rabbit, chicken, guinea-pig, gerbil (if you keep domestic rats as pets, it's OK to put their cage cleanings on the compost heap; the scent won't attract wild rats – they will detect that there are rodents already in residence and move on elsewhere).

Avoid:
Perennial weeds
Roots or large clumps of perennial garden plants
Seeding annual weeds
Seedheads of invasive garden plants, e.g. poppies, foxgloves
Meat and fish waste or scraps
Carnivorous animal manures

'**Brown**' materials are dry, tough and slow to decay.

Add:
Cardboard and newspapers, if scrunched up into balls about 6in (15cm) diameter
Straw sold for animal bedding from a reputable source
Autumn leaves from healthy trees
Hedge prunings and clippings from healthy, non-prickly shrubs, not more than 1/2in (1.5cm) diam-eter; if very long, chop into 12in (30cm) lengths
Shredded or chipped healthy hedge cuttings or tree prunings
Woodshavings and sawdust from untreated timber
Wood ash from bonfires, or spent charcoal from bar-becues (when firelighters or accelerants are not used)
Clean cotton or wool rags

Avoid:
Plastic, glass, rubber or metal
Glossy magazines, waxed or shiny paper
Diseased plant material (*see* Chapter 8 for what is safe to compost)
Wood over 2in diameter, or painted/treated wood
Prickly shrub prunings
Oily, creosoted or other material known to be con-taminated
Hay (it contains large amounts of weed seeds)
Cloth made from artificial fibres
Coal ash and clinker

Homemade compost bin: one chamber to rot and one maturing.

are reasonably long lasting, even using untreated timber, and often their contents degrade quicker, being better aerated and less inclined to condensation than plastic.

If you're on a tight budget, probably the cheapest, if not the prettiest compost container is made from four substantial posts knocked into the ground, securing pallets onto these with binder twine, or nailing a section of wire netting round on three sides, with the last side having wooden planks or a pallet for easy access.

The contents of these more open style bins will not decay so well at the sides, as the the centre will retain heat but the outside will be cold, so for best results they should be turned at least once. If you don't want to go to the effort of turning insulate the sides using a thick layer of cardboard. The inventive can devise all sorts of variants according to whatever material is cheapest and readily to hand, recycling anything from industrial conveyer belting to breeze blocks to hold the compost.

Unless you garden on a limestone soil, garden compost is inherently acidic, and regular use over a number of years will lower the pH of soil. If this is becoming a problem, either scatter a small quantity of ground limestone over several layers of the compost as you construct it, or apply lime directly to the soil as part of crop rotations.

MUNICIPAL COMPOST

Municipal compost is made from garden and commercially produced 'green' waste (e.g. prunings from tree surgeons, apple pulp from cider makers, lawn mowings from sports grounds) stacked in immensely long heaps called windrows. The material is turned mechanically every week for at least fifteen weeks, and very high temperatures are achieved, killing off weed seeds, pests and diseases. When composting is complete, the result is screened to remove any plastics or large uncomposted matter, graded for texture quality, then bagged up and sold to the public, often at a budget price.

Municipal compost tends to be relatively high in potash, and has lower levels of nitrogen and phosphorous compared with homemade garden compost: it often can be acidic, pH 4.5–5.5. Municipal compost is excellent used as a mulch on borders or as a potting compost ingredient being free of weed seeds, or dug in as a soil conditioner.

If you have a really tiny garden, or one mostly down to shrubs, a local council garden bin or bag scheme can be very useful. Such schemes normally involve buying special plastic bags or renting a green bin for material which you can't or don't want to compost at home, such as particularly prickly prunings.

A mulch of municipal compost will retain moisture around this Acer.

WORM COMPOSTING

Worm composting is a method suitable for people with very small gardens, who have mostly kitchen waste to dispose of. If you're not used to them, worms can at first appear to be fiddly and demanding, but once you have become accustomed to the difference in methods, worm composting can be very rewarding.

Brandling or tiger worms, Eisinella foetidia, *are one of the principal detritivores found in compost heaps.*

Unlike ordinary earthworms, which dislike damp warm decaying matter, the compost worms or brandlings (*Eisinella foetidia*) and red worms (*E. rubra*) are native debris feeders which graze on surface leaf-litter. They quickly convert organic wastes to a high quality compost with marvellous texture.

A collection of worm bins.

Worms need a temperature of 50–77°F (12–25°C) to work, and are most efficient without large fluctuations between day and night. To give them the correct conditions, either keep their bin in a warm shed or garage during the winter, or insulate their home well before the cold weather starts (insulation can be as simple as wrapping an old carpet or a double layer of bubble-wrap round the bin).

When starting a worm bin, you can buy a purpose-made one or make your own from a dustbin. Drill holes in the base, and fill the lower third with clean gravel. Make a plywood disc which will fit the inside of the bin, sitting on the gravel, and drill holes in it to allow excess moisture to drain. Put in a deep layer of shredded paper or cardboard, which the worms will use as bedding material (you can also use leafmould or composted chipped bark).

Then add the worms, which can be bought by mail order from various suppliers or dug from another worm heap or compost heap. You will need around 1000 if you intend to buy them, or at least 2 pints (1000ml) volume of live worms if you have collected them yourself. Scatter a thin layer of worm food such as fruit or vegetable peelings, tea leaves or crop waste over the top and cover with a damp newspaper. Put the lid on the bin and leave for a week before adding any more food.

Worm bins are not – or shouldn't be – smelly, and if they become stinking, something has gone badly wrong. Check the drainage, and add more bedding material such as newspaper. If you can't see any worms, and the bin contents are putrefying, it may be that the worms have died – clean the bin out (you can safely put the contents onto a normal compost heap) and start again. Worms may die off during a cold winter, or from being neglected, but it's safer to leave your bin unfed over a holiday rather than give them extra and risk overfeeding.

An occasional problem in the summer, especially if you are being rather generous with fruit peel is the appearance of masses of tiny black fruit flies, which aren't harmful, just irritating. Add more newspaper and cut down on the fruit waste for a while.

Collecting worm compost from the bin without

DOS AND DON'TS WITH WORMS

Do:
Make sure your worms have adequate drainage, as they release a large amount of liquid – if using a bought worm bin, leave the tap in the open position; add the liquid you collect to a conventional compost heap rather than applying it directly to plants.

Add plenty of adsorbent, cellulose rich material in the form of newspaper, shredded paper, paper bags or cardboard regularly.

Feed your worms once a week in small amounts – no more than a half bucketful at a time; they enjoy fruit and vegetable peelings, cooked vegetarian leftovers, coffee grounds and small quantities of green waste such as annual weeds.

Add eggshells regularly (or a little ground limestone once a month).

Remember to move the bin indoors or insulate it in cold weather – and remove the insulation when it's hot!

Don't:
Worms don't eat dairy products, bought flowers (often treated with preservative or pesticides), meat or fish, or lawn mowings; they dislike large amounts of citrus peel too, as this is over-acidic.

Don't overfeed the worms by adding too much food in one go.

Don't keep worms at the wrong temperature – site bins out of direct sun, draughts and rain.

Don't allow drainage holes to become blocked.

Don't worry if all the worms have come to the surface – this is often caused by changes in atmospheric pressure, so check again in a few days; if they are still at the surface, check for other problems such as being too wet or overfed.

Don't worry if you can't see any worms – provided the food is regularly disappearing, they will have just moved further down the bin to more comfortable conditions.

Don't allow local anglers to raid your worms for fishing bait!

losing all your worms might at first seem an insoluble problem, but in reality it's a simple job which just takes a little time: to harvest the contents of a dustbin full of worms allow a bright sunny afternoon.

Empty the bin's contents onto a sheet of plastic or a slabbed patio, and spread it out in a layer about 2in (5cm) thick. Put a piece of damp cardboard about 18in (0.5m) square over the compost in one corner, and go away for some hours. The worms will have collected under the cardboard, so shovel up the compost immediately under it and return them to the bin, complete with fresh bedding. Repeat this procedure if necessary, to reclaim as many worms as possible: they will die if moved onto ordinary garden soil. Expect to harvest a smaller quantity of worm compost than from an equivalent sized garden compost bin.

Worm compost is higher in nutrients than garden compost, and is weed free, so it's ideal for use in a potting mix or as a top-dressing either for container plants or greedy feeders such as courgettes, roses and dahlias.

LOVELY LEAFMOULD

Leafmould is one of the best soil conditioners in existence, and regular use over time will both increase the volume, texture and inherent fertility of the soil.

Leaves are low in nutrients but high in humus and contain massive numbers of micro-organisms, so provided you have sufficient quantity it can be applied in large amounts. Apply as a thick mulch, to a maximum depth of 4in (10cm).

Leafmould's soil-building effect can be shown clearly in a demonstration area at Ryton Organic Gardens, where a patch of ground which was formerly grazing land has been treated in the same way every year for over twenty years. One third has been cropped without any additional input, one third has been cropped with leafmould applied every autumn and one third has had a green manure sown, with a subsequent crop grown on it. The soil which has been treated with leafmould is now substantially higher than the others, and looks darker, crumblier and better draining. Plants growing on it are healthier and more productive than the green-manured plot, which in turn is higher and more productive than the area cropped alone.

Making Leafmould

Rake up healthy deciduous fallen leaves when slightly damp, and either stack them in a wire

Eighteen-month-old leafmould...

...comes from trees like these.

netting container or stuff them into a black plastic bag, tying the top, stabbing with a fork to make a few holes and leaving in a corner for a year. The easiest way to collect the leaves is by mowing the lawn with the mower set on its highest setting, which breaks the leaves into smaller particles and mixes them with a little nitrogen-rich grass for quickest decomposition.

Some local councils are mechanically collecting roadside leaves and allowing their drivers to deposit them at convenient sites for the public to access, such as allotments or community gardens.

Roadside leaf sweepings are now safe to use, as unleaded fuel is the norm, but such collections often harvest large amounts of litter as well as leaves. Contact your council to see if there is an area near your home where you can obtain pre-collected leaves.

Year-old leafmould is a joy to handle, containing few weed seeds and fewer pests. It adds bulk to homemade potting composts, is invaluable for a top-dressing for container plants and makes an excellent addition for ground intended for growing root vegetables: unlike manure or garden compost it doesn't cause forked root development in carrots and parsnips.

If you have diseased trees, such as apples or pears with scab, it is quite acceptable to add their leaves either to a hot compost heap or to a pile of leafmould which will be used elsewhere in the garden, at least 20yds (6m) from a tree of the same species.

COMFREY AND OTHER PLANT EXTRACTS

Comfrey (*Symphytum spp*) is a family of mostly deep-rooted perennial plants, many species having leaves rich in potassium and trace elements. After an exhaustive series of tests by Lawrence Hills, the most productive species was found to be the Russian hybrid comfrey *S. x uplandicum*, the cultivar 'Bocking 14' being the best for garden use. This cultivar has the dual advantage of not setting seed or spreading invasively by runners, unlike other species, and has the highest levels of potassium in its foliage. It is widely grown by organic gardeners as a self-perpetuating source of potash.

A single clump of comfrey will take up the same area of ground as a rhubarb crown – approximately one square yard/metre – and requires generous applications of garden compost to perform well. Maximum nutrient levels are reached in the plant just before the flowers open. Leaves and flower-buds can be cropped four times a year, cut off at ground level.

Comfrey leaves and stems can be added directly to the compost heap, placed as a mulch around established shrubs such as fruit bushes or made

into comfrey liquid, which is a useful homemade tomato and container plant feed. When handling comfrey leaves always wear gloves, as their rough hairs can be a skin irritant.

ABOVE: *Russian comfrey 'Bocking 14'.*

BELOW: *Comfrey leaves and their result, a bucket full of comfrey liquid.*

Making Comfrey Liquid

There are several ways of making comfrey liquid. The easiest one is to fill a large container with comfrey leaves, top up with water, cover it and leave undisturbed for two weeks until the liquid has turned dark brown. This comfrey tea can be diluted with water (1:10) as a continuous feed for young plants, or applied in equal parts with water weekly once plants have matured.

To make a more concentrated plant food, fill an empty waterbutt with comfrey leaves only, pressing them well down with gloved hands or by treading, but add no water. Cover the butt, leaving the tap closed. After a few days the leaves will have begun to decompose, and a dark brown smelly liquid will drip out once the tap is turned on. This is liquid comfrey extract, containing at least 5 per cent soluble potassium compounds. Dilute 1 part comfrey extract with 15 parts of water and apply to container plants twice weekly. Feed tomato plants regularly with comfrey once the second truss of fruit has set.

If not required immediately, comfrey liquid can be kept for use in plastic containers, but do not fill these over two-thirds full, as secondary fermentation can occasionally cause stored bottles to explode. Do not keep beyond the end of the current growing season: any surplus should be poured onto the compost heap, where the valuable nutrients it contains can be recycled.

Other plants can be used as a natural source of soluble feeds. The problem weed marestail (*Equisetum* spp) is high in silicates and trace elements. If the leaves are boiled for ten minutes and the liquid allowed to cool it can be used undiluted as a plant tonic.

Nettle tea is made by soaking nettle leaves for a week or so in a bucket of water, and while not particularly high in food value, the tea contains beneficial micro-organisms and acts as a probiotic for plants. Like marestail extract, nettle tea should be used undiluted whenever plants are stressed by climate conditions, prolific flowering or fruiting or pest attacks.

Stable manure… a possible worry for gardeners.

FARMYARD MANURE (FYM): THE CASE OF THE CONTAMINATED CROPS

For many years the key to a good fertile soil, particularly for growing vegetables or flowering shrubs such as roses, has been regular use of well-rotted farmyard manure. Manure in itself is not particularly rich in nutrients, but the microbial health of the soil and its texture is greatly improved following its application. Manure water, made by collecting a hessian sackful of sheep-droppings and steeping it in a waterbutt, was long used as a source of nitrogen for potted plants.

Gardeners are becoming increasingly reluctant to use manure, following recent use of a persistent broad-leaved weedkiller by farmers, which has led to serious adverse effects on plant life. The problem developed when fields used to grow either grain crops or pastureland were treated with aminopyralid, a herbicide first used in 2006 in a particularly long-lasting formulation to destroy weeds in grass or grain. When the crops were cut, and the straw used for animal bedding, or hay made from the treated meadows, the chemical was still intact and fully operational.

Manure from animals which had been fed or bedded on contaminated hay, silage or straw was toxic to plants, especially vegetables, even after stacking the muck for twelve months. Characteristic effects are elongated pale, stunted

NUTRIENT LEVELS IN MANURES

These are approximate levels, as a percentage of dry weight. They vary somewhat according to the individual animal and its diet.

Animal	Nitrogen	Potassium	Phosphorus	Ratio of dry to fresh weight
Rabbit	2.7	1.5	0.9	14:1
Horse	1.7	0.6	1.9	24:1
Dairy cow	2.7	1.1	2.5	48:1
Pig*	1.0	1.3	1.8	38:1
Chicken	2.2	1.0	0.8	21:1

*Most pig feeds now contain appreciable levels of copper as a growth adjuvant, so pig manure is not recommended as a long-term addition to soil because of the possible danger of accumulated toxins.

growth and curled leaf ends, particularly noticeable on potatoes or tomatoes, with plants completely failing or sometimes never emerging from seed-sowing. Similar effects can occur with related chemical herbicides, including chlorpyralid, which is sold for use on domestic lawns. Vegetables, particularly tomatoes, potatoes, beans and lettuce are worst affected, as well as roses, raspberries and strawberries, while sweetcorn, hard-barked shrubs and trees are relatively unscathed.

Following a public outcry, aminopyralid has been banned in the UK, but at present it is unknown how long aminopyralid is likely to persist in the soil, or how far down the food chain it has progressed. The problem has been present in soils for at least three years, although other long-lasting herbicides are known to degrade over time under attack from soil bacteria. As hay may be stored in reasonable condition for up to three years, and manure stacked for two years does not appear to have lost its toxicity, the problem is not over yet, although things should be improving by 2012.

In the immediate future, gardeners are recommended not to use farmyard manure from animals from a source they are not completely confident is free of aminopyralid contamination. Risk-free

Phacelia tanacetifolia, a summer green manure which is loved by bees.

sources include horse or sheep droppings collected from animals grazing solely on untreated pasture, pigeon coop cleanings or poultry droppings from birds kept on sawdust. For maximum security, use manure or straw from farms which are certified Organic, but expect to pay a premium for it.

GREEN MANURES

Green manuring is the practice of improving the soil by growing a crop which is dug in at any stage of growth before it flowers. There are two types of green manure: the fertility building legumes, which improve nitrogen levels from root-living bacteria, and nutrient holding or saving crops, which prevent leaching of minerals from the soil by covering it with a growing crop until about two months before sowing time.

The benefits of green manures can take a long time to become visible, but will greatly improve the soil over several years. In the short term, after green manures have been recently dug in there may be nitrogen deficiency in the soil as the decomposing bacteria multiply, and germination inhibitors may be present in the soil for some weeks afterwards. It is usual to sow modular grown plants or large seeds such as peas, beans or cucurbits as the first crop after green manuring to lessen these effects.

Green manure	When to sow	Length of use	Benefits
White clover	April–July	Long term: 6 months minimum; can be left for several years	Nitrogen fixing Tops can be cut for compost ingredient Bee fodder Weed suppressant
Fenugreek	May–September	Half-hardy summer only: lives 6–10 weeks	Nitrogen fixing Small amount can be removed as herb Weed suppressant
Winter tares	August–October or February–May	Winter hardy: lives 3–5 months	Nitrogen fixing Tolerates drought Weed suppressant
Field beans	October–November or February–May	Winter hardy: lives 3–6 months	Nitrogen fixing Can act as windbreak
Alfalfa	May–August	Long term: not always winter hardy; ideally lives 2 years	Nitrogen fixing Tolerates drought Cut for compost occasionally
Lupin	April–July	Winter hardy: lives to 18 months	Nitrogen fixing Deep roots bring up buried minerals and break up soil
Crimson clover	April–June	Half-hardy summer only: lives 3–5 months	Nitrogen fixing Valuable bee fodder Attractive flowers
Trefoil	April–June	Lives 5–9 months but can be left up to 2 years	Nitrogen fixing Drought tolerant Bee fodder Weed suppressant
Buckwheat	April–June	Half-hardy summer only: lives 3–6 months	Bee fodder Weed suppressant
Grazing rye	March–October	Winter hardy: lives 6–9 months	Deep roots break up soil Weed suppressant Fertility holding
Phacelia	March–October	Usually but not always winter hardy: lives 3–7 months	Fertility holding Bee fodder Attractive flowers
Mustard	March–October	Winter hardy: lives 4–6 months	Fertility holding Bio-fumigant

Fenugreek, a nitrogen-fixing green manure, is also used in Asian cooking, where it is called methi.

Sowing a green manure is a good method of dealing with ground that you have cleared but haven't got time to dig thoroughly or plant: while you are concentrating efforts elsewhere, your soil is benefiting from improved aeration and drainage from deeply penetrating roots, and additional fertility.

Many of the more vigorous species when sown thickly form dense mats which squash out annual weeds, while a long-lived green manure such as white clover will weaken many perennial weeds including dandelions and nettles, if these are cut back regularly once they appear, to give chance for the clover to overwhelm their crowns. Long-term green manures can be cut two or three times a year, using a strimmer or shears, and the tops put on the compost heap. Cutting back regularly will increase root activity and boost their soil improving potential.

Mustard in particular has bio-fumigant properties, where the sulphur-rich compounds released by the roots of the growing plants destroy pests in the soil. Similar compounds are released from the leaves as they decay once the manure has been dug in, while these effects persist over a subsequent growing season. If growing green manures in the vegetable patch remember that all the legumes are in the same rotation group as beans and peas, while mustard is a brassica.

Large packets of green manure seeds are available from many seed merchants, and increasingly more garden centres stock the common species. Some enterprising companies are offering smaller trial packets, so you can experiment with a new species on your soil.

Lastly, even if you don't manage to dig in all your green manures, the frost-tender species can be happily left to flower through the summer and delight beneficial insects. Clover, buckwheat and *Phacelia* are all favourite flowers with native bumble bees, which are becoming rarer in the countryside due to intensive agriculture, while hoverflies and parasitic wasps are also frequent visitors. Should you want to sow an attractive flowering mixture which will also have fertility benefits, try the 'Tubingen Mix', a selection made by a German university for maximum insect feeding potential as well as soil-improving qualities.

Before digging in perennial green manures such as clover or alfalfa, smash the tops down with a spade to hasten decomposition. Try to ensure total soil inversion (i.e. all the tops are completely buried) when turning the crop in.

Composting is not a particularly unhygienic process, but some common sense precautions should be observed when dealing with large quantities of decaying material. The main dangers are from bacterial infections to cuts or inhaling fungal spores, which can give rise to long term problems such as farmer's lung. Disposable face masks can provide some protection but become constricting to use when working hard and breathing deeply, when the maximum number of spores would be taken in. Open wounds should be covered or, at the very least, well-washed after handling compost, and care should be taken to avoid inhaling spores from a newly uncovered or dusty heap. Don't use or turn compost or leafmould in a confined space, and turn your face away when removing a lid from a compost bin. And obviously, wash your hands before eating!

I've been working as a professional gardener for the past 28 years, and find when I first work in a new garden that all minor cuts and scrapes become infected for a day or two, then I become immune to infection for even quite deep wounds, however dirty they get. This immunity lasts for about 25 years, and takes around a day to re-establish itself. 'New' gardens seem to be ones separated by distance – usually around a mile on a similar soil and age of garden – or soil type, not how they are worked (organic/non-organic, or heavy manuring v. no manure) or by what they grow.

CHAPTER 5

Plants for a sustainable garden

Most gardens need to import a substantial amount to keep them running well, from new plants, bulbs or seeds through soil treatments in the form of manure or artificial fertilizers, to plant supports from netting to string.

Some of these are necessary, some less so. With planning, even a small garden can become more self-sufficient, ecologically attractive and less dependent on chemical or other additives. While making your own string may not appeal (although *Phormium* leaf strips are very handy for tying up the odd trailing tendril), it is possible to grow some of your own garden sundries. This could be as simple as using some of your twiggier prunings to prop plants up, instead of buying bamboo canes.

As gardens increasingly become smaller, we demand plants which have multipurpose value, being attractive throughout the seasons, or feeding us as well as looking good. The ideal plant for an ecological garden should not only fulfil these categories but be non-invasive, disease resistant, require little if no upkeep and be the correct plant type for the site. So before you reach for a spade, consider, 'Will this plant be happy growing here? Why am I growing this? What can it do for my garden?'

Species which are disease resistant or unattractive to pests can be selected for by long-term selective breeding, or in the case of a particularly vulnerable species by growing a close relative which is immune from attack. For example, rust attacks the common hollyhock, *Althaea rosea*, but less so *A. ficifolia*, the fig-leaved hollyhock, while

Hazel tree underplanted with Crocus thomasinianus, Primula vulgaris *and* Anemone nemorosa *is not only beautiful…*

…but functional too, as prunings provide plant supports.

the species *Althaea pallida*, *A. rugosa* and *A. taurica* are virtually immune. Unless the genetic base for resistance is caused by several genes, over time the organisms which are responsible for the problem will gradually develop tolerance, so read your seed catalogues regularly to select newer cultivars with maximum disease-free potential. Fruit and vegetables are most likely to be selected for resistance, because of the demands of commercial growers, but there are other improved forms of many good garden plants which are healthier than their original cultivars.

APHID-FREE RASPBERRIES

During the past twenty years several UK raspberry cultivars were bred to be resistant to the four species of aphids which carry raspberry viruses. If you plan to grow on a site which is likely to be attacked by aphids, perhaps on an allotment, select one of these cultivars for longest productive life. 'Malling Augusta', 'Julia', 'Juno', 'Minerva' and 'Gaia' are resistant to all four aphid species. 'Malling Promise', 'Malling Admiral', 'Orion' and 'Glen Ample' are resistant only to some, not all aphids. 'Glen Doll', 'Glen Garry', 'Glen Magna', 'Glen Moy' and 'Glen Prosen' also have good aphid resistance.

TREES

Even a very tiny garden needs a small tree or large shrub – it gives form and height to the surrounding space, shelter from the sun and a song-post or nest site for birds.

Flaking, textured trunk of a mature Betula jaquemontii.

If you or your insurance company are concerned about tree roots damaging foundations, there is a new method of containing the roots in a semipermeable bag made from a copper-impregnated geotextile. The small feeding roots can penetrate the bag, so the tree can survive but larger roots are restricted, giving a dwarfing effect. So far, it does not appear to have made them any less stable in high winds. As an example, a walnut tree grown in this manner will achieve about two-thirds less of the expected size in ten years than one growing in open ground.

If you're prepared to wait a little, why not grow your own trees or shrubs? You can propagate a large number of species from seed, and most cultivars will reproduce some if not all offspring similar to their parents, provided you sow enough. Children especially can become very involved with growing their own trees. It's always very satisfying to watch as something you raised from seed finally outgrows you, knowing that with luck it will live to be enjoyed by your grandchildren.

Try looking in the larger seed catalogues such as Chilterns for inspiration, or see if you can exchange seed at a local horticultural association or garden club meeting. Some larger organizations, such as the RHS, distribute free seeds to members annually, and this enables gardeners to have access to unusual plants at very little cost except postage and packing.

The UK is remarkable for having one of the widest ranges of plants growing in gardens open to the public anywhere in the world, from large stately homes to splendid public parks. Don't be tempted to just take seed without asking permission first – it genuinely is stealing and may rob dedicated staff of their only chance to propagate a rare plant for several years. I know from personal experience how professional gardeners live in fear of eager amateur gardeners stealing propagation material from their prize plants, but they are quite happy to allow you to collect a few fallen berries or seedpods to try at home, provided you request permission. You might even come away with cutting material or rooted seedlings if you ask!

Once you've collected your seed, remove any fleshy berry parts by putting it in a plastic bag with a handful of sharp grit, scrunching it up and

THE GOOD NEST GUIDE

The following trees are favoured by these birds for nesting.

		Birds
Small trees	Apple	mistle thrush, woodpeckers, finches
	Birch	song thrush, blackbird, greenfinch, collared dove
	Cherry	song thrush, blackbird, greenfinch, collared dove
	Elder	mistle thrush, whitethroat, blackcap, wren, goldcrest, linnet, finches
	Holly	blackbird, long-tailed tit, dunnock
Shrubs, climbers and hedges	Berberis	blackbird, long-tailed tit
	Box	greenfinch, goldcrest, dunnock
	Cotoneaster	song thrush, blackbird
	Conifer hedges (including *x Cupressocyparis leylandii*)	blackbird, collared dove, spotted flycatcher, starling
	Hawthorn	blackbird, song thrush, blackcap, whitethroat, long-tailed tit, linnet
	Honeysuckle	goldcrest, blackcap, long-tailed tit
	Ivy	song thrush, blackbird, spotted flycatcher, long-tailed tit, goldfinch, chiffchaff, wren, dunnock
	Sloe	whitethroat, blackcap, finches, collared dove

Magnolia sargentiana.

squishing between the fingers, then put in a jam jar of water – the flesh floats to the top while ripe seed sinks. Collect these, and sow in a pot or tray of soil-based compost. Topping with grit helps deter weed seeds, and covering the top with fine-

gauge wire mesh prevents blackbirds or mice from digging in the pots. Leave in a sheltered place in the garden over winter and wait until spring before you can expect to see the first shoots emerge. Some seeds can take two seasons to germinate, so if nothing happens, keep the pot watered over the summer and leave it for another year.

Be bold with your seedlings if they all come up. A group of birch seedlings can look spectacular as a short-lived planting. Take out the weakest over five to ten years to provide beanpoles, lineprops or firewood, and enjoy the vertical design of different sizes of long pale trunks.

TREES FOR GARDENS

Suitable small to medium sized trees for gardens of 60–80 sq yd (30–40 sq m) could include any of the following (all of which can be raised from seed, although they may differ from their parents):

Acer campestre, A. micranthum (*A. palmatum* and *japonicum* in sheltered sites)

Amelanchier (all)

Betula jaquemontii, B. papyrifera, B. pubescens, B. pendula, B. utilis

Corylus avellana and *C. maxima*

Crataegus pinnatifolia major, C. opacea, C. azarolus

Malus (all)

Sorbus aucuparia and *S. aria* (fastigate cultivars and most of the ever increasing hybrid population, such as the columnar *S. aucuparia* 'Bessneri', will not breed true and should be propagated by grafting or cuttings)

Taxus baccata

When selecting larger plants which will take a long time growing as well as valuable space, think about their alternative uses as well as their appearance throughout the year. What will you need to do in the way of pruning, and can you make use of the stuff you cut off – how much will you be able to use in the garden, or woodburner, or will it all have to be transported to the local tip? For example, a magnolia looks magnificent in flower but has little value for wildlife, and its large leathery leaves are slow to decay, while a birch or amelanchior is more value for money, giving not just a spring display but beautiful autumn colour as well as food for birds, while smaller leaves break down rapidly for leafmould. Short twiggy birch boughs will help prop up floppy perennials and longer branches will make more substantial plant supports, while magnolia wood is resistant to decay so thin branches can be used for longer-term (lasting at least two or three seasons) garden structures.

SHRUBS

Everything mentioned in the tree section applies equally to shrubs, but a careful selection of shrubs can be delicious for the tastebuds as well as other senses. For example, *Cornus mas* flourishes in heavy clay soil, tolerates lime and bears tiny, fragrant yellow tufts of flower in early February, before producing red Cornelian cherries, good for pies or jams if you pick them before the birds, early in July. The short densely twiggy growths make for good nest sites and plant supports. Roses, particularly many of the species roses, are not only beautiful but tasty in flower, although the white base of

ABOVE: *The pink-tinted flowers of* Sambucus *'Black Lace' can be made into elderflower champagne.*

BELOW: Rosa rugosa *has large and delicious hips for making preserves. Rosehips are also popular with blackbirds.*

each petal should be removed as it can be bitter. *Rosa rugosa* is one of the best, flowering prolifically enough that you can bear to remove some flowers and still be left with enough for a good display of blooms and large rosehips for making jam or syrup.

SHRUBS FOR EDIBLE BERRIES

These are some less common shrubs with edible berries or fruits (which may need cooking first):

Buffalo currant *Ribes odoratum*
Elder *Sambucus nigra, S. canadensis*
Japanese dogwood *Cornus kousa*
Judas tree *Cercis siliquastrum*
Salmonberry *Rubus spectabilis*
Szechuan pepper *Zanthoxylum piperitum*
Shrubby honeysuckles *Lonicera angustifolia* and *L. caerulea*

Foliage from *Yucca, Corydalis* and *Phormium* can be used in place of string, as can hop-bine, *Clematis* or *Lonicera* stalks and the stems of strong-growing perennials like *Lathyrus latifolius* or various grasses: *Calamagrostis, Stipa* and *Miscanthus* are all good. Picked and tied when young enough to be supple, then allowed to dry tighter, they should last for a growing season, and of course don't need to be removed as they are fully biodegradable.

Try to choose shrubs to prolong the flowering period as much as possible, to please not only yourself but any passing insects who drop in for a quick snack. Winter flowering plants are often fragrant rather than showy: even on a dull damp day, enjoy the scent of *Lonicera x fragrantissima* 'Winter Beauty', *Hamamelis mollis, Daphne mezereum* or *D. laureola*.

HEDGES

Shrubs chosen for hedging should be slower growing, so as to only require clipping once annually. To minimize disturbance to nesting birds, trim non-fruiting hedges from late August onwards, or fruiting ones once the berries have been devoured in autumn.

Native hedging plants sloe *Prunus spinosa* and hawthorn *Crataegus monogyna* and *C. oxycantha* were principally chosen because they're common, easily grown from seed, tolerate pruning well and are stockproof, armed with stout thorns. In smaller gardens you may wish for a slightly less vicious barrier: Berberis is often recommended for burglar deterrence, as are holly *Ilex* and *Pyracantha*. All are attractive in flower or fruit and are capable of being trained tightly to a boundary fence or wall. Don't plant them close to the back of a border or you will be equally deterred from weeding once you've encountered a few stray prunings.

The most ubiquitous hedge is probably the

Berberis x logonensis *'Apricot Queen' looks good, keeps the bees fed in flower, deters intruders and has berries for the birds later – what more could you want?*

dreaded 'Leylandii', which according to where you live can be applauded or loathed. Yes, it's cheap, quick growing and does well almost everywhere, but unfortunately it doesn't know when to stop, with a potential height of over 150 ft (50m), is fatal to most things growing next to it by starving them of water and air, and can itself be subject to a sudden death even when well established, due to severe attacks of conifer aphid. If you are happy to remove over 3ft (1m) of growth annually and enjoy plenty of exercise climbing ladders, then no doubt *x Cupressocyparis leylandii* is the hedge of choice for you.

Box, while currently fashionable is not always long-lived, being permanently stressed by being made to perform unnaturally as a hedge. A box tree in the wild can reach 7ft (2.2m) or so in height, considerably more across and can live over a hundred years with ease – small wonder that the tight clipped, overcrowded and often starved bushes which make up knot gardens die so rapidly!

Deciduous hornbeam *Carpinus betulus* and beech *Fagus sylvatica* look similar, with both retaining their bronze-orange dry foliage all winter, and grow at roughly equal speed, but hornbeam will require much greater effort to trim, having harder wood than beech. Against this it is hardier and more drought tolerant, doing well where beech won't survive.

Other non-prickly possibles for evergreen hedging include yew *Taxus baccata*, the indestructible cherry laurel *Aucuba japonica, Prunus lusitanica* and *Thuja plicata*.

Unless you're keen on frequent hedge cutting, avoid the low-budget horrors of *Lonicera nitida*, privet *Ligustrum ovalifolium* and *x Cupressocyparis leylandii* which can need trimming several times a season.

HERBACEOUS PERENNIALS

These have been the mainstays of the classic English garden for over a century now, and are still deservedly popular. The ideal plant self-seeds easily without being invasive, and is easy to transplant or pull up when it's growing where it's not

ABOVE: *It would be a wicked waste to eat the flowers of these* Allium *'Purple Splendour', but they are delicious additions to a salad, tasting like a mixture of garlic and chilli.*

BELOW: Crocus speciosus *'Conquerer' supported by* Festuca glauca, *a beautiful combination for a woodland edge.*

needed. It should be beautiful in flower, scent or taste, attract a wide variety of insects and need little if any heat to get started from seed. This may sound like impossible to achieve but most cottage garden plants possess just these attributes, which is why they have persisted so well through years of cultivation.

If you want something a little different, try the blue-purple tubular flowers of *Dracocephalum grandiflorum* or dragonhead, which will bring the bees buzzing all summer to its floriferous domes. Other good plants for attracting bees, both hive and wild, include *Lysimachia clethroides*, balm *Melissa officinalis*, pennyroyal *Mentha pulegium* and its relatives *Mentha x piperata*, *M. spicata*, and *M. citrata*, and the butterfly magnets *Oreganum laevigatum* and *Pycnanthemum pilosum*.

BULBS

Gardeners rarely think of devouring flowering bulbs, although we don't hesitate to eat onions. Many of the species we cultivate for their beauty are edible in whole or in part, although care should be taken to have identified the correct species before eating.

Alliums are always useful in the garden as an emergency food supply, regardless of their beautiful flowers, although it would be a waste to pluck some of the better hybrids just because you'd run out of chives. Some species shouldn't be allowed in through the gate, being alarmingly invasive. Steer clear of the ground-swamping *A. moly*, or even worse *A. triquetrum*, as well as the native ramsons *A. ursinum*. Other edible bulbs include *Camassia*, *Erythronium* and *Lilium tigridium*.

Tulips have delicious flowerpetals, which make a different, if extravagant, addition to spring salads.

Birds occasionally visit flowering bulbs as well as insects: one of the first recorded instances of a British bird ever feeding on flowers successfully was observed when bluetits were seen visiting *Fritillaria imperialis* to devour the hanging nectar drops.

Calendula or English marigold.

A FEW SOUND ANNUALS

These annuals all have insect attractant flowers.
(* with edible flowers and/or leaves)

Baby blue eyes *Nemophila insignis*
Californian poppy *Eschscholzia californica*
Candytuft *Iberis umbellata*
Coriander *Coriandrum sativum**
Cosmos bipinnatus and *C. sulphureus*
Erigeron karavatense 'Profusion'
Foxglove *Digitalis spp*
Honesty *Lunaria annua*
Mignonette *Reseda odorata*
Nasturtium *
Flowering tobacco *Nicotiana* (all)
Poached egg plant *Limnanthes douglasii*
Pot marigold *Calendula officinalis**
Rudbeckia (all)
Scabious (all)
Sunflower *Helianthus spp** (unless you're a hayfever sufferer, avoid the pollen free sunflowers, as they don't set seed – they're no good for birds or bees)
Sweet alyssum *Lobularia maritima*
Sweet rocket *Hesperis matronalis* *
Viper's bugloss *Echium vulgare* and hybrids

GRASSES

A large number of butterfly larvae feed on native grasses, including skippers, small copper, marbled white and speckled wood. Sadly, these species are likely to come to the garden to feed but not lay eggs, being attracted to large grassy expanses (road verges, hayfields or unmowed derelict land) rather than finely cut turf interspersed with longer clumps. You may try to encourage their breeding by leaving strips of long grass at hedge bottoms uncut until spring, but don't expect them to be permanent residents as a rule.

Grass left rather long, up to 2–3in (5–7cm) between mowings, or trimmed from midsummer onwards is a vital home for voles and shrews. When clearing long grass, before using a strimmer do walk through the sward waving a long stick to disturb the grass and warn off frogs and any other small creatures, as accidents often happen and are distressing for all parties.

Miscanthus stems make marvellous firelighters and can be used in place of raffia for temporary plant ties. The more dexterous can indulge in all sorts of grass-weaving crafts, making anything from straw hats to mats or baskets.

ABOVE: *Flowerbuds of Japanese wineberry,* Rubus phoeniculatus.

BELOW: *Blue nettle-leaved bellflower,* Campanula trachelium, *has edible flowers and young shoots, while golden* Doronicum *is a good early summer nectar source for bees.*

Ipheion uniflora *has edible flowers and foliage, and survives anywhere sunny. It's an ideal woodland edge plant.*

FOREST GARDENS

Forest gardens are based on the observation that the most productive area in nature is the edge of a woodland, with trees, shrubs and lower plants all flourishing as a community. The idea of a forest garden is to combine the multiple layers of height in a productive habitat which requires minimum input from the gardener but gives maximum output of mostly perennial edible plants, even if these are not the most common or usual vegetables. It implies the gardener reverts to a version of our nomadic gathering ancestors, encouraging plants rather than suppressing them, as in conventional horticulture.

A forest garden can work very well, but the area it is based on needs to be free of perennial weeds. Careful management is required throughout its lifespan, which can be extensive, involving tree removal or major thinning. In some situations, such as a shady inner city garden, incorporating ideas and plantings used in a forest garden may be the only way of harvesting anything edible from a problem plot. Invasive plants can be used with care in a forest garden, as their extra vigour will mean quicker recovery after cutting for food, but they shouldn't be allowed to take over.

Forest gardens are created with wildlife in mind as well as people, so within the planting there should also be provision for nest sites, holes or other habitats, such as log or brushwood piles, and butterfly larval food-plants, to establish maximum biodiversity and thus reduce pests.

For more information on making and managing forest gardens, see Robert Hart's excellent book on the subject, *How to Make a Forest Garden*.

A pile of logs makes a good refuge for all manner of creatures, from hedgehogs to newts.

Suitable Plants for a Forest Garden

Location	Type	Examples
Upper stories	Fruit trees Nitrogen-fixing trees Timber/shelter trees (these will need to be coppiced as they grow to useable size)	birch, hazel, medlar, quince, apple, *Gleditsia* (nitrogen fixer), *Acer pennsylvaticum* (timber and sugar from sap)
Middle stories	Fruiting shrubs Edible flowering shrubs Large herbaceous perennials	*Rubus phoeniculatus* and related species, gooseberry, black and red currant: *Rosa rugosa*, *Sambucus spp*, *Cercis siliquastrum* (edible flowers and pods), *Semiarundinaria fastuosa* (edible young shoots, bamboo canes, windbreak), Jerusalem artichokes
Lower levels	Edible roots, leaves, flowers and bulbs Small fruits	*Hemerocallis*, *Allium cernuum*, dandelion, *Campanula portenschlagiana* and *C. poscharskyana* (edible flowers and leaves), wild strawberry, Turkish rocket (*Bunias orientalis*)

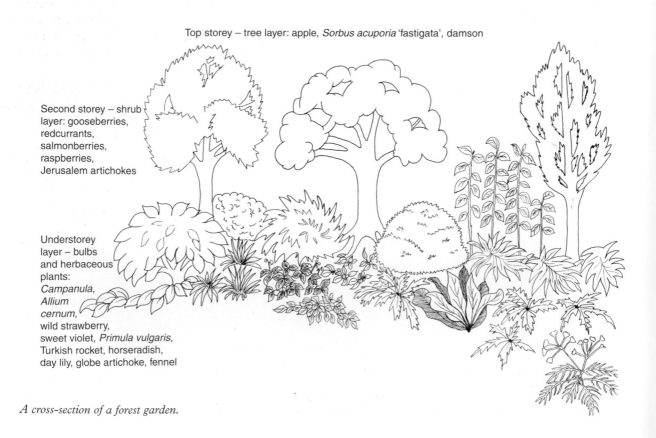

Top storey – tree layer: apple, *Sorbus acuporia* 'fastigata', damson

Second storey – shrub layer: gooseberries, redcurrants, salmonberries, raspberries, Jerusalem artichokes

Understorey layer – bulbs and herbaceous plants: *Campanula*, *Allium cernum*, wild strawberry, sweet violet, *Primula vulgaris*, Turkish rocket, horseradish, day lily, globe artichoke, fennel

A cross-section of a forest garden.

PLANTS FOR A PRAIRIE GARDEN

Classic Plants

\# dry sites
* damper sites

Achillea millefolium (all) #
Agastache foeniculatum, A. anisata
Aster laterifolius
Calamintha nepeta #
Coreopsis grandiflora, C. lanceolata
Echinacea purpurea and *E. pallidiflora* (but not the modern orange or yellow hybrids which are more frost-tender)
Gaura lindheimeri #
Geranium macrorrhizum #, *G. endressii,*
G. psilostemon #, *G. renardii* #
Gillenia trifoliata #
Heleniums

Iris siberica, I. germanica
Libertia perigrinans
Linarea purpurea 'Cannon Went' *or* 'Alba'
Perovskia atriplicifolia
Phlox paniculata
Polygonum affine, P. bistorta, P. vaciniifolia
Rudbeckia
Salvia farinacea, S. nemorosa, S. pratensis #
Solidago #

Prairie Grasses

Anaemanthele lessoniana, syn.
Calamagrostis x 'Karl Foerster'
Eragrostis elloittii, E. spectabilis
Miscanthus cultivars
Molina caerulea *
Panicum violaceum and cultivars *
Stipa arundinacea

PRAIRIE PLANTINGS

Prairie plantings, where a mixture of grasses is interspersed with bold perennials, was originally popularized by the designer Piet Oudolf, and has rapidly become established as a flowing, naturalistic design often found in modern urban greenscapes.

A successful prairie scheme may be as labour intensive, if not more so, as a similar area of shrubs and bulbs, for at least six months of the year, and requires substantial inputs of mulching material periodically to keep down weeds, if not planted through a geotextile. If a geotextile is used, the weed problem is greatly diminished, but the capacity of a large plant population to adapt to weather

Miscanthus sinensis
flowerheads flow on a windy day.

Annuals can add to the impact of prairie planting, especially in the early years when the perennials have yet to fully establish. Here Perovskia atriplicifolia *contrasts with glowing* Helichrysum bracteum monstrosum *in autumn light.*

conditions will be less. When plants are allowed to self-seed, one or two species will be prominent in a wet season, while other species dominate in a drier year, but there should be background levels of seed reserves to deal with, whatever climatic extremes develop.

The ever-changing growing display, with associated attractions for wildlife from flowers and seed make it a very attractive option for blurring boundaries between dwellings, such as open frontages for a group of houses or flats, rather than a main feature for a small domestic garden. A raised bed or other clearly defined area planted with a prairie style mixture can look extremely striking, yet be easily controlled.

Once planted out, a prairie planting should be cut to ground level once annually, usually just before the growing season starts. This will give you an opportunity to remove intrusive weeds, thin down invasive species and divide plants to maintain vigour, as well as renew the mulch if necessary, using low-fertility, long-lasting material such as bark chippings rather than the traditional gravel. Weed removal will need to be continued at least fortnightly until the mulched area is no longer visible.

COPING WITH A CHANGING CLIMATE

The weather has always been variable, but in the last few years there seem to have been greater extremes in climate than previously. When global warming was initially observed, UK gardeners believed that climatic areas might slip upwards from the Equator, giving us a Mediterranean climate with hot dry summers and warm wet winters, and that in decades to come olives or citrus fruit might fruit outdoors as plentifully as apples do now. So far, this hasn't really happened except in the mildest parts of the UK (although it is possible to have an occasional small crop of olives from your own tree, if you have a very sheltered garden, and lemons can be fruited in a conservatory). The trend appears to be simply greater fluctuations in existing weather patterns, particularly with rainfall: but at least for now, the winters are becoming warmer.

Outside, keeping susceptible plants well-drained is vital to avoid frost damage to roots: many will tolerate sharp frosts provided their roots aren't in waterlogged soil, and if their crowns are protected by a thick layer of large leaves or bracken, enclosed within a chicken wire cage, that may be all the protection they need. The real danger comes from uncertain spring weather, which tempts buds in February to break prematurely with a few mild days then blasts the shoots in March with an icy spell. One of the best methods to diminish the danger of this harming your plants is to divide a new plant as soon as possible, then grow the divisions on all around the garden, so that a few emerge late from more shaded or colder positions, surviving winter chills. Routine applications of organic matter during the year will boost humus levels, increasing moisture retention in drought, and encourage a healthy root system to bind the soil during summer downpours.

One of the main sources of carbon dioxide polluting the atmosphere is domestic heating, and there is very little justification now for the ultimate luxury of a greenhouse heated all winter long. If tender plants are grown year round, they have to be capable of surviving with very little extra heat, or be small enough to live on windowsills indoors during the winter.

Should this mean that the ecologically conscious gardener is limited to growing native species, or those which require no additional heat at all in any part of their lifecycle? Probably not: if the climate changes as rapidly as is forecast, growing plants with the widest possible tolerance of extremes may be vital for our survival as a species.

Limiting our growing habits to plants which require frost-free conditions to survive winter may be a better choice, or perhaps growing things which only need limited protection to develop from seed. Endless production of thousands of annual half-hardy bedding plants is clearly not a long-term option, being the nearest thing yet to throw away gardening: but growing a single long-lived potted lemon or peach, if you are lucky enough to have a glass porch or similar space where it can be placed in cold weather, might well be justifiable.

The ideal is a probably a bulb or tuber, which can be potted up and left in a mouse-free garage or shed, or a larger deciduous plant, kept in a similar frost-free place over winter; once cut hard back, it will shoot afresh in spring. Fortunately, there are a large number of species which fill these criteria, from *Mirabilis* and *Pelargonium* to *Brunnsmagia*,

Salvia elegans or *Lippia citrodora*. You will have to weigh up your own situation and consult your conscience about what, if anything, you can keep going through the winter months.

THE JUNGLE GARDEN

Tropical planting schemes are being increasingly used by urban gardeners, where large plants in a small space can conjure up an image of flourishing jungly wilderness, giving welcome privacy and shade. Most of this effect can be achieved with hardy plants, with a few carefully selected tender plants which can be brought into shelter during the cold. Cities are not only warmer and more polluted than the surrounding countryside but often have pronounced wind-tunnel effects, often up to gale force, especially between large blocks. Careful choice of plants to grow can diminish these wind-tunnels, benefiting everybody in the neighbourhood.

For a wind-resistant garden, try a filtering living bamboo screen of *Phyllostachys nigra* (confined in a deep-buried container, such as a concrete drainage pipe or copper-impregnated membrane, if you have a heavy clay soil) or the less invasive *Fargesia robusta*. Both of these are attractive to small birds as shelter. The larger *Phormiums* will also give an upright windbreak, as well as privacy, but present similar problems of spread. Smaller cultivars such as 'Maori Maiden' are easier to manage.

Bold leaves and extra height can be added by *Aralia chinensis*, whose flat heaped flowerheads are filled with nectar, or any of the slightly shorter tree paeonies with dramatic foliage, changing colour constantly through the growing season. Fill in the gaps with golden *Choisya* 'Sundance' or *Fatsia japonica*. In damp spots add *Ligularia*, *Darmera peltata*, *Rogersia pinnata* or *Hosta sieboldiana*, with *Rudbeckia pinnata*, *Agapanthus*, coral coloured fern *Dryopteris erythrosa* and *Sanguisorba tenuifolia* in drier places. Suitable annuals include *Amaranthus* (all species have edible leaves), *Venedium arctosis* and *Madia elegans* whose leaves smell exotically fruity when bruised, with climbing nasturtiums, *Ipomoea*, *Martynia* or *Thunbergia*.

CHAPTER 6

Growing fruit and vegetables

Growing your own fruit and vegetables is one of the most rewarding and satisfying things you can do in your garden. It is claimed that there are now more people growing their own food than at any time since World War II, and most major seed companies say their vegetable seed sales have exceeded that for flowers for the past few years.

It needn't be backbreaking work, although you will have to put some effort in, especially during the early stages. After you've tasted the rewards of your labours, you'll appreciate any effort made is well worth the rewards in flavour and freshness.

FRUIT

If you only have limited space, consider growing tree or top fruits, which can be grown to fit almost any shape and size, using a variety of training methods such as cordon, espalier, fan or arch. They will take a couple of years to come into full bearing but will then crop well for the next twenty years and more, requiring little save for a twice yearly prune.

Apples and pears can be trained into a hedge alongside the boundary of a vegetable patch, while plums or cherries can be trained on a wall as a fan. Either of these methods will take up no more than 30in (80cm) of depth, but up to 12ft (4m) in width and 6ft (2m) in height.

Favourite Fruits

During the depressed days of the 1970s, the choice of fruit cultivars in the UK became very

The perfect vegetable garden?

Cordon apples. Note the flowering bulbs beneath, to induce bees to visit the orchard.

limited, and many old local apples were in danger of becoming extinct. With the advent of groups like Common Ground and the Marcher Apple Network, added to the 1980s foodie culture, fruit growers responded by finding and propagating old varieties again. We are currently in a golden age of fruit growing, with more cultivars for sale than at any time since the Victorian era. The earliest apples don't keep, so are best grown as cordons, which limits the size of crop, so you don't become surfeited with a glut.

Apples

Here are just a few cultivars to get you started.

Early eaters	'Discovery'	Tastes best straight off the tree
	'Worcester Pearmain' 'Mother', syn 'American Mother'	Tolerant of alkalinity Great aromatic flavour
Early cookers	'Rev W. Wilkes' and 'Emneth Early'	Make very compact, slow growing trees, so shouldn't be grown on a very dwarfing rootstock
	'Golden Noble'	Matures a little later; good flavour
Midseason eaters	'Suntan'	Will grow well where Cox won't, although it tastes similar
	'Ribston Pippin' (one of the parents of Cox) 'Ashmead's Kernel'	Richly aromatic flavour Needs to be stored for six weeks before eating
	'James Grieve'	Big, acid fleshed apple for those who prefer juicy scrunching; can double as a cooker
Late eaters	'Tydeman's Late Orange'	Great eating in January; good colour
	'D'Arcy Spice'	A russet which can last even later
	'London Pippin'	Old, hardy
Late cookers	'Warner's King' 'Wellington'	Good for mincemeat or apple pies; yellow-greenish

Late apples are not so popular nowadays – who has a cellar or lofty attic room to store much fruit? But if you are lucky enough to have a north facing spare room which can be kept just frost-free, then consider 'Tydeman's Late Orange', 'D'Arcy Spice', or 'London Pippin'.

Mid to late season cookers don't have to be the ubiquitous Bramley – try 'Warner's King' or 'Wellington', known as 'Dummellor's Seedling' in its native Leicestershire (although the pedantic RHS insists it should be called Dummellow's).

Pears

Sadly, the great apple revival in cultivars has not extended so far to pears. Of the myriad of cultivars formerly known, we have only a couple of dozen

Some butterflies, like this comma, will feed on surplus fallen fruit as it decays.

remaining which are widely grown now, apart from the ubiquitous 'Conference'. This may be because pears are often thought to be more difficult and demanding to grow than apples, or simply that they don't keep well so can't be stored.

Pears don't like wet feet or cold winds, and if subjected to adverse conditions won't produce quality fruit. Apart from preferring slightly warmer, drier growing conditions, pears are as easy to cultivate as apples.

Most of the older pear cultivars need a pollinator, but both this and the problem of storage can be avoided by growing as cordons or espaliers. It's easier to grow a cordon against a wall, which acts as a storage heater, protecting fragile blossom against spring frosts or encouraging fruit to ripen in a cold wet summer. Good recent cultivars to try are self-fertile 'Beth', 'Concorde' and 'Merton Pride'.

Plums

Plums are less popular than they formerly were, again perhaps because they make a large tree and don't store well once ripe. Plums will always need more room to grow in than apples or pears, but modern cultivars, careful choice of rootstocks and selective pruning can give a productive tree for a confined space.

Some of the most popular fruits of former times are notoriously shy to fruit in poor conditions. They are perhaps best regarded as ornamentals, with any fruit as a bonus. Most of the delectable gage plums behave like this, cropping consistently in the home counties but often only producing a dozen fruits annually when grown further north.

'Opal' makes a fairly compact tree with medium sized, early, golden fruits. The old 'Warwickshire Drooper' is also fairly small growing, while the early 'Blue Rock' can be extremely prolific.

Damsons are tougher and more resilient than plums, so are better suited to less favoured sites:

although there are several different cultivars there is little to choose between them, all being blue-black, intensely and sharply flavoured.

If you live on a bleak windswept hillside, it may be worth cultivating cherry plums, a variant of *Prunus cerasifera*, as a windbreak. Long grown in France as mirabelles, these small, ultra hardy fruits are ready in late July, and make excellent jam. The early flowering trees are thorny, utterly hardy and grow almost anywhere: they are wind, frost and stockproof. Choice is limited, although some nurserymen are now importing French cultivars such as the marble sized 'Mirabelle de Nancy'.

Cherries

Cherries seem to be replacing plums in popularity as garden fruit, especially as many of the recent dessert cultivars such as 'Stella, 'Summer Sun' and 'Sunburst' are self fertile. A cherry tree in fruit will always need protecting from the birds, so decide how you will support and secure netting before you plant one.

What Rootstock?

Apples, pears and almost all other tree fruits are grown from small pieces of the original tree (the scion) grafted onto a rootstock, which determines the size and vigour of the resultant tree.

All modern rootstocks are represented by an initial and a number. For example, 'MM' indicates the 'Malling Merton' strain, used for designating woolly aphid resistant rootstocks, and '106' which indicates the size the tree will grow to.

The effect of a rootstock on the tree's growth is not the only factor which determines how large the tree will become – some cultivars are naturally dwarf, e.g. apple 'Rev. W. Wilkes' and pear 'Beth' while others, especially triploids such as Bramley, are much more vigorous. (Triploids are plants which possess extra chromosomes, and are often heavier cropping or have larger fruits than normal. They usually require at least one other normal chromosome plant to fertilize their flowers.) Soil fertility and site exposure will also influence tree size. If you have a poor soil or a challenging site it's best to select a tree on a less dwarfing rootstock.

Plum 'Opal' is a regular cropping early cultivar that does well even on indifferent soils.

COMMON ROOTSTOCKS USED TODAY

Apple

Rootstock	Size	Result	Gardening advice	Best use
M9	Very dwarfing	Produces a short-lived but very precocious small bushy tree with large fruits	Needs lifetime staking or other support Unsuitable for exposed or wet sites Requires a fertile soil to perform well Frequently forms an unsightly burr round the base of the tree at the graft union, which may sucker if damaged by a careless hoe or strimmer Useful cropping declines after about twenty years	Ideal for cordons
M26	Dwarf to semi-dwarfing	Produces a slightly larger and longer-lived tree than M9	Doesn't always need support Better cold tolerance than M9, and less liable to form suckers	Suitable for espaliers, cordons, bush trees Good in pots
M27	Very dwarfing	Often produces smaller fruit than M9	Always needs a stake Won't tolerate neglect Resistant to replant disorder	Ideal small tree for containers or cordons
M116	Medium to moderate vigour (a new rootstock released in 2001)	On poor soils produces a dwarf tree (where M9 would probably die) On good soil can be double the size	Tolerant of a wide range of conditions and longer lived than M9 or M27	

Pear

In the UK pears are grafted onto Quince rootstocks (*Cydonia oblongata*) while in the rest of the world, especially the USA, pear seedlings of known vigour are used. Quince A and C are both dwarfing and shallow rooted, so don't suit very exposed sites. Quince A is slightly earlier to begin cropping. A new Quince rootstock, EMH, was released in 2001, which is said to encourage large fruit on the stock it is grafted onto. Pear seedlings do better on inferior land, as they tolerate a wide range of conditions and poor soils, being deep rooted and sturdy, but take several years to produce a first crop. In the USA, Bartlett and Brooklyn rootstocks are used, while in Europe the 'Day' series is popular, along with Adams.

Plum and Cherry

Rootstock	Type	Size	Gardening Advice
Gisela 5	Dwarfing cherry rootstock	Tree grows to 10ft/3m	Heavy, consistent crops Early to come into fruiting Better frost hardiness than Colt
Colt	Semi-dwarfing cherry rootstock	Tree grows about 15ft (5m) tall	Resistant to replant disease
Pixy	Dwarfing plum rootstock	Produces a precocious tree about 10ft (3m) tall, but reduces fruit size	Shallow rooting, so not good for dry areas

Patio Fruits

As the climate appears to be changing to warmer, wetter conditions during summer and less severe winter frosts, more people are turning to potted fruits. These have been grown in the UK for centuries but only for the very rich. Now, with the growing number of conservatories and sun rooms, anybody can have a peach, apricot or fig tree of their own.

Peaches, nectarines and apricots fortunately come in genetically dwarf strains, such as peach 'Garden Lady' or 'Bonanza', as well as normal sized trees. The dwarf forms stay small enough to be mobile – remaining in a 16in (45cm) diameter pot for many years – so provided you've got a

Young peaches, about the size of a walnut, which now require further thinning to a single fruit.

sturdy sack barrow to shift them, move tubs to a frost-free area during cold times of year, usually after Christmas. Remember that some chilling is necessary for flowerbud formation, so only transfer them to cover if forecasts are for –7°C or below before the New Year.

If you keep stone fruits protected from over-head rain in spring while the leaves are unfolding, they escape the unsightly effects of peach-leaf curl disease and can be safely placed outside later when they are no longer susceptible to infection. Keeping rain out also excludes insects, however, so you will have transfer pollen between flowers. Anything can be used – a soft brush is often recommended, but equally well suited are a pussy-willow flower or even the tail of a co-operative cat! Hand pollination will mean that rigorous thinning will be required later, or the tree will be overloaded with tiny, misshapen fruits. Don't expect more than about a dozen full-sized peaches from a small potted tree, so thin accordingly, no matter how tempting the fruit set looks.

Figs need rigorous control in their root systems, or they will only grow leaves, not fruit. A full-grown fig should never be allowed to have a root run of much over a cubic yard/metre or it will never produce a crop. Restrain the roots by using a 20in (47cm) maximum diameter container – but make it strong, as figs can easily deform a thin plastic pot as they try to escape their confines.

Figs actually produce two types of fruit, the larger ones which develop in late summer and usually come to nothing being frosted during the winter, and tiny embryo figs which develop during the spring to ripen fully in midsummer. To assist these embryos in ripening it's usually recommended that all of the larger figs are removed before winter in the UK. The most planted cultivar is probably 'Brown Turkey', although 'Ischia' and 'Violette Hative' are also becoming popular.

Weed Control in Fruit

Mulching with old newspaper and straw helps plants by reducing weeds and conserving moisture. If you want to feed them as well, it's easy enough to do so at the same time: spread a layer of FYM or compost over the roots just before applying mulch.

When the soil is damp, in late May, cover the area below the plants with overlapping newspapers. Don't separate into individual pages, just unfold along the centre spread, then scatter a 4in (10cm) layer of straw over the top to keep the paper weighed down. Allow at least 12in (30cm)

Fan-trained fig 'Brown Turkey' growing on a sunny south-facing wall.

each side of a row of raspberries, or a 3ft (1m) circle around the base of a standard apple tree. If you haven't got straw you can use a thin layer of grass mowings – less than 2in (5cm) deep at a time – and repeat every time you mow the lawn.

In winter, remove the mulch and compost it. Leaving the soil beneath the bushes bare for a few months is important, to let the weather and birds find and destroy any bugs or disease spores lurking over winter. Hanging a well-stocked bird-feeder up in your bushes or trees helps too – birds will search for insect food as well as what you provide.

Don't be tempted to apply the mulch too soon in the year: if you insulate the soil on a night when the air is colder than the surrounding soil the bushes may get frosted.

Soft Fruits

Soft fruit plants will last for over ten years, so start off by buying good plants from a reputable nursery or catalogue – avoid supermarket cheap offers or a few offsets from a neighbour. Be particularly careful with second-hand or unusually cheap raspberry plants as they are almost certain to be infested with virus. Paying the extra for government certified stock really is worth doing, as these are guaranteed disease free.

Raspberries are probably one of the heaviest cropping fruits for the space they take up – every 12in (30cm) length of established raspberry canes should yield at least 1¼lb (600g) of fruit a year. A raspberry row will be productive for at least twelve years. To grow raspberries you need a well-drained site which has direct sunlight at least half the day in midsummer. They don't like growing in a pot, however large!

The canes will need some sort of support to stop them being damaged in strong winds and to make the fruit easy to pick. A simple T-shaped wooden support carrying two wires erected every 10ft (3m) or so along each row will enable the canes to be tied in to a permanent post at each end of the row. Arching down the canes encourages fruit production by slowing the flow of sap, stimulating flower-buds to grow in preference to leaves.

Good modern summer fruiting cultivars include 'Octavia', 'Minerva', 'Glen Ample' and

Straw mulch for fruit trees at Ryton Organic Gardens.

'Tulameen'. As the canes stop producing fruit, cut them down and select up to five stout substitute canes from the new growth around each plant to fruit next year.

Autumn raspberries are ideal for gardeners with little time, as they only need to be cut down to the ground in January, and supported once the canes have grown. They will crop from August until the frosts. Recommended cultivars include 'Autumn Bliss', 'Joan Squires' and the yellow-fruited 'Fallgold'.

Strawberries take a little more care, needing to be replaced by runners every few years, but this can be accommodated into a vegetable patch as part of rotations. There are regular or summer

White currants are not so well known as their red cousins but they taste equally good.

Blueberry foliage and fruits in autumn.

strawberries, fruiting once only, or 'everbearers' which flower and fruit twice a season. Everbearers usually have the heaviest crops, but as this is spread over several weeks they may not have as many fruits all ripe at once as the summer berries. This can be a good or bad thing depending on how you prefer to eat your fruit, either as massive jam making and family munching sessions or continual grazing.

Blueberries are hot crops at the moment, because of their superfood status – they're supposed to be good sources of almost everything healthy!

For most people blueberries are best grown in pots, as they need a damp acid soil. If they get too dry the berries drop, so regular watering is vital. Use rainwater wherever possible for irrigation. If you have to use tap water, add an occasional feed of sequestered iron or chelated seaweed extract, especially if you notice the leaves turning an unhealthy yellow or you live in a hard-water area.

Blueberries are delightfully decorative as well, having flowers opening before reddish or orange leaves in spring, as well as a flaming autumn display before returning to coloured twigs over winter. A single blueberry bush should crop over 2lb (1kg) annually after a few years if grown in a container, but will need another plant of a different cultivar as a pollinator. Top-dress the pots using spent conifer needles to encourage the growth of beneficial mycelium. Spruces (*Abies*) and Pine (*Picea*) are said to be best. Don't pick the berries until the thin red line at the stalk has vanished, or they will taste unbearably sour.

Gooseberries are tough spiny survivors – long-lived and extra-hardy, they'll grow almost anywhere. They can cope with exposure to wind or frost, chalk or pollution.

A gooseberry likes lots of root room so will only last a few years even in a big container. Any method you can train an apple you can try with a gooseberry – flat fan or espaliered against a wall, a standard or as vertical cordons. Summer pruning the laterals from these spurs, like a cordon apple, will increase fruiting potential the next season.

Sadly, the best flavoured gooseberry cultivars are prone to mildew and often prickly. 'Invicta' is mildew resistant but viciously thorny. 'Whitesmith' is an old favourite, early enough for pies and afterwards sweet for dessert. Red 'Lancashire Lad' is mildew resistant, as are the rather tasteless but thorn-free 'Pax' and 'Hinomaki Red'. Perhaps the most delicious flavoured is the splendid red dessert 'Whinham's Industry', a martyr to mildew – so grow it as a cordon or fan to allow ample circulation of fresh air.

Red (and white) currants are an almost forgotten fruit in the shops, but well worth a place in even a tiny garden. They will tolerate being in a pot for about five years if the initial container is large enough. Like gooseberries they can be grown in all sorts of elegantly trained forms to take up minimal space. Pruning hard will produce bigger, if fewer berries. A full-sized mature currant bush should give 11lb (5kg) fruit a year or more. Redcurrants will cope with some shade, provided they receive at least five hours sunshine daily in the summer.

Blackcurrants demand a good soil, but are very productive and pick easily. They're much cheaper to grow than buy. They are greedy feeders and relish regular dollops of compost or FYM. You can't grow a blackcurrant easily as a cordon or fan so they're best just as a bush – and they loathe being in a pot!

Grow a blackcurrant bush in an open, but not wind-blasted, position with moisture retentive soil which doesn't waterlog in winter. It should grow productively for at least ten to fifteen years. Expect anything up to 8lb (3.5kg) per mature plant. Pruning is easy – as soon as you've planted one, chop it to ground level to encourage plenty of strong growth, then after the third year remove about a third of the older wood annually. Old stems are dark coloured and show up best in early spring before the leaves open. Lazy gardeners with room for more bushes can practise the type of pruning used commercially for juice production, where one plant is chopped to ground level every three years while the others are left untouched.

Blackberries or hybrid berries are one of the most productive ways to utilize a wall or fence. Many of the spikiest sorts have superior flavour, proving that you don't get something for nothing in the plant world.

Blackberry cultivars include thornless 'Chester' with pretty pink flowers like tiny roses, followed by wild-tasting berries, and the old ornamental 'Parsley Leaved,' which crops consistently in cooler areas. If you have a lot of space to cover, consider the well-armed 'Fantasia' which can spread 20ft (6m) easily in a single season, with freezer-filling crops of monster berries.

There are many hybrids between blackberries and relatives – boysenberries, tayberries, loganberries and more! Like blackberries, they come in thornless and thorny cultivars. Pruning is relatively easy, similar to summer raspberries. Tie in developing canes to one side until fruiting has finished, then cut out old stems.

VEGETABLES

Vegetables can be grown even in a small space at home or, more commonly in these days of ever-diminishing back gardens, on an allotment or community garden.

For those who have very limited space, try growing in containers. Probably the best known type of container is the humble growbag, but almost anything can be pressed into service from disused oil cans to washing machines.

If growing in large or deep pots – perhaps an old barrel or dustbin – it's vital to have a well-drained compost which isn't too heavy, as roots will not penetrate deeply if the soil becomes too compacted by overwatering. Use a loam-based rather than peat compost as it will retain water better. Well-composted bark or leafmould is a suitable addition as is vermiculite, rather than grit or sharp sand, to improve drainage. The ideal compost for growing in these conditions should resemble coarse muesli, with a range of particle sizes, rather than fine breadcrumbs.

Vegetables suitable for pots include runner and climbing French or kidney beans, radicchio, cut-and-come again lettuce or other salad crops, spinach, Swiss chard and leaf beet, mini sweetcorn, kale, cucumbers grown upright on a support and celery if very well-watered. Peas grown in pots almost always seem to grow much taller than they do in open ground, so make sure you have a good support system.

Square Foot Gardening

The square foot garden is an idea developed by Mel Bartholomew. It aims to grow the maximum produce from a minimum of land using little effort, and provided you have somewhere else to raise plants (a windowsill will do fine) it does just that. I practised a square foot garden for over four years and found that it grew a small amount of vegetables very well – during the summer I had something to pick every week for two people, sometimes three, from a single demonstration square foot plot.

The basic format is a 4ft (1.3m) square divided equally into 16 smaller squares by string or bamboos laid along the soil, allowing at least 18in

Allotments show vegetable growing at its best.

A Square Foot Garden

Garlic × 9	Potato 'Swift' × 1	Cabbage 'Greyhound' × 6	Parsley × 4 Chives × 2
Leaf beet perpetual spinach × 5	Cress curled, 2 rows Calendula × 2	Leek 'King Richard' × 16	Broad bean 'The Sutton' × 3
Radish 'Scarlet Globe' × 16	Kohl rabi 'Purple Vienna' × 9	Lettuce 'Little Gem' for cut & come again	Turnip 'Veitch's Red Globe' × 9
Peas 'Sugar Dwarf Sweet Green' 2 rows × 4 = 8	Peas 'Sugar Dwarf Sweet Green' 2 rows × 4 = 8	Potato 'Swift' × 1	Lettuce 'Cockarde' × 6

An example of what could be grown in the square foot garden during spring

Plants are grown closer together than normal, and picked as soon as they possibly can be, thus giving more space to the remainder. As soon as a 12in (30cm) square gap appears, it must be replanted or resown with another crop. Up to five crops a year can be obtained from individual squares, and as you can imagine, rotation becomes a lesson in horticultural ingenuity – a vegetable version of Rubik's cube! Maintenance is very easy and quick compared with an allotment or traditional veg patch, and the biggest problem is slugs or snails because of their impact on such intensive growing.

Rotation

Plants belonging to each other, or related in their family groups take up similar nutrients and are attacked by the same range of pests including invisible ones such as nematodes or viruses. This means that yields suffer if the same group of plants is grown on the same place year after year. To avoid this happening, move related plants around the vegetable patch every growing season.

Plants like peas and beans add to the soil by fixing nitrogen from their roots, while others such as brassicas deplete certain nutrients, so by moving crops round, the gardener helps the soil retain its fertility. Different soil treatments will benefit some crops more than others, but all will slowly improve your soil both by adding nutrients and benefiting the soil structure. Potatoes and onions benefit from manure, for example, but this makes root crops such as carrots and parsnips develop multiple roots, so don't treat the soil intended for carrots during the twelve months before sowing.

The important thing is not to grow the same type of plant on the same ground year after year. Equally, you don't have to cultivate what you don't like eating. If you hate all members of the cabbage family, don't grow them – plant wallflowers or stocks instead and grow your vegetables in the flower beds or in growbags that year.

Simple Crop Rotation

Year 1	Year 2	Year 3	Year 4
Potatoes (Manure)	Brassicas (Lime)	Onions (Compost)	Legumes
Brassicas (Lime)	Onions (Compost)	Legumes	Potatoes (Manure)
Onions (Compost)	Legumes	Potatoes (Manure)	Brassicas (Lime)
Legumes	Potatoes (Manure)	Brassicas (Lime)	Onions (Compost)

An example of a simple crop rotation, adding garden compost, lime if required and well-rotted farmyard manure.

(45cm) surrounding access on all sides. This area is claimed sufficient for one person's food during the growing season. The soil must be of the best quality available – it should be prepared by digging in compost or well-rotted manure, and after every crop is removed some sort of additive, even if only leafmould or potting compost, should be put back.

Growing Families of Vegetables

Plants from the same families may be prone to the same pests and diseases, have similar nutrient requirements and prefer the same methods of growing. They don't all look alike, so it's helpful to know what's related.

Vegetable Families

Vegetable	Family	Latin name
Potato, tomato, aubergine	nightshade	Solanaceae
Cabbage, kale, Brussels sprout, turnip, oriental brassica, kohl rabi, mustard	brassica	Cruciferaceae
Pea, bean, asparagus pea, fenugreek	legume	Leguminosae
Onion, shallot, garlic, leek	onion	Alliaceae
Lettuce, Jerusalem artichoke, chicory, salsify and scorzonera	sunflower	Compositae
Beetroot, spinach, leaf beet or swiss chard	beet	Chenopodiaceae
Carrot, parsnip, parsley, coriander, fennel, celery, celeriac	carrot	Umbelliferaceae
Cucumber, melon, marrow, pumpkin	pumpkin	Cucurbitaceae
Sweetcorn, corn salad	(unrelated plants which can fit in anywhere)	

How to Grow

The following vegetables are suggestions, given in the order of what's easiest to grow. There are of course many other possibilities.

Potatoes

Potatoes are divided into *earlies* which take around 10–12 weeks to mature, *second earlies* taking 14–28 weeks and *maincrop* which take over 20 weeks. The maturity is affected by day length as well as temperature. Contrary to what the old boys on the allotment may tell you, potatoes don't 'clear the ground' – you do while growing them! When was the last time you saw a spud with a fork in its hand?

Early potatoes should be planted 12in (30cm) apart allowing 2ft (60cm) between the rows; maincrop 18in (45cm) apart and 3ft (1m) between rows; and second earlies at distances in between.

Potatoes do best in a rich, fertile soil, with a generous helping of manure or garden compost added to it before planting, or as a follow-on crop from a green manure such as field beans or grazing rye. The plants can tolerate a little shade but must have good drainage.

Avoid the main risk of potato blight by growing *first earlies*, to enjoy your delicious freshly dug new potatoes when they're at their most expensive in the shops.

Always buy certified seed potatoes, preferably of the higher quality 'Super Elite' or EC1 grades. Never be tempted to plant some old tubers left over from the kitchen which have started to sprout. They'll bring pest and disease problems with them which may last a very long time.

Frosts will kill early growth, so delay planting during cold spells. If your potato foliage is only just visible above ground and a frost's forecast, draw a little soil over the tops – if plants are too big to

Potatoes can be a rewarding crop but require an amount of effort.

do this, then drape them with horticultural fleece or old curtains or cover them with newspapers for the night.

Earthing up (drawing soil around the tops of the potatoes so that only a small amount of foliage sticks out) is useful in stimulating tuber development for maincrop and second earlies. If you can't earth up because of close spacing, then pile well-rotted garden compost, leafmould or even straw on top of the plants instead.

Early cultivars can be harvested from mid June in a favoured site, through to late July, when the second earlies start to come along. Maincrop cultivars should be dug when the leaves are dying down in autumn, usually before October. Allow them to dry off before rubbing excess soil from them and storing in sacks in a cool, dark frost free place with good air circulation.

Tomatoes

You can grow tomatoes from seed on a windowsill or buy in plants from a nursery. Growing from seed gives a much better range of fruit size, shape and colour – anything from lime-green striped with yellow to almost black.

If you grow your own, for plants in the open sow a few seeds in a pot or in modules from late February to mid March, and keep at a temperature of around 60°F (16°C) or slightly higher. Once big enough to handle, prick out into larger pots and keep growing on in light but cool conditions.

Plants will probably need potting on again before gradually accustoming them to fresh air outdoors

Tomatoes are just one of the plants that have large numbers of heirloom varieties, saved by dedicated growers worldwide and rarely being commercially important.

and planting outside when the danger of frosts is past. They'll need a sheltered position, away from strong winds, in full sun.

For container growing, you can fit three tomato plants to a growbag, or one large plant in a 12in (30cm) pot. Remember that plants in containers will need lots of regular watering! Tomatoes in containers should be fed weekly with a high potash feed, such as comfrey liquid, once fruit has formed, but if grown in open ground, with reasonably fertile soil, plants don't need extra feeding.

Some tomatoes are naturally bushy (non-determinate) while others grow tall and lanky (determinate) so require slightly different growing methods. Bush tomatoes are generally left to themselves, and just propped up with a few twigs, while determinate plants should be grown as cordons up a string or cane to ensure maximum earliness and large fruit size, pinching out side shoots and only allowing six or seven trusses of fruit to set.

Tomatoes will keep about a month if picked slightly unripe, and will ripen over a longer period when picked green. To encourage ripening, put a banana or ripe pear in a plastic bag or closed drawer with some of the green fruit, which will release ethylene gas, a stimulant which increases fruit maturation.

Onions from Sets, Shallots, Garlic and Leeks

Onion sets are small immature bulbs which are planted in spring or autumn. Growing from sets is much easier than from seed, although the result won't reach the immense sizes seen on the show bench.

If you have a dry sandy soil it's probably best to

go for autumn sown sets, while on heavy clay land spring sown ones are recommended. Onions need a fertile soil, with good light and adequate drainage. They don't like being crowded.

Sets need a cold spell to initiate root formation, so plant as soon as the soil is workable, from March till April in spring, or September to November in autumn. When planting sets, push the bulb, pointy end upwards, into the soil sufficiently that you can just see the top. For normal kitchen use, space 4–6in apart, while autumn sown plants should be at a slightly wider distance. To produce bigger onions, double the spacing.

Onion roots are shallow, so hand weed carefully. If you notice any of the plants starting to flower, pull them up and use immediately – red onions are particularly prone to this, especially if temperatures or water intake fluctuates.

You can harvest an onion from any time it's big enough to eat, but obviously biggest bulbs develop when the plants have stopped growing and the leaves are starting to fall over naturally. As the leaves wither, pull up the plants carefully and set them on a slatted bench or tray (indoors in wet weather) in a single layer so that the skins can ripen to rustling dryness. Onions can be stored in string bags, tied up in ropes or spread in boxes in a dry, airy place (doesn't have to be dark). Use any damaged or thick necked bulbs first.

Shallots are small onions which grow many bulbs from a single set. They are usually milder tasting than onions, even easier to grow and quicker to mature, but need wider spacing. Allow at least 8–12in (10–12cm) between plants. Shallots are usually sown in spring but in mild areas or very light soils can be set in November. They store very well and keep longer than onions.

Garlic is also very undemanding but needs a long growing season. There are two methods of planting garlic: the conventional, which assumes you will use dried bulbs, or the Asiatic, which harvests the 'green' or wet garlic.

Buy garlic bulbs specifically for planting rather than for food – this not only reduces the risk of importing diseases onto your plot but also ensures that you will be growing a plant adapted to UK, rather than subtropical, conditions.

For the largest bulbs, plant individual cloves from early November to late December, pushing each one (pointy end up) at least 2in (5cm) deep into the soil so that they are completely covered, unlike shallots and onions, spacing 8in (20cm) apart between plants. You can also plant garlic outdoors in February to March, but don't expect such heavy yields.

Keep plants weed free and when the leaves are starting to die down mark the rows. Dig up when leaves are withering and dry off in the same manner as onions. Don't panic if the garlic flowers while growing – this doesn't affect their cropping.

To grow green garlic, push cloves in only shallowly, 1in (2.5cm) deep and 3in (7cm) apart, in rows, allowing 4–5in (9–11cm) between each row. As soon as the garlic is big enough to use, crop alternate rows.

Leeks are very hardy, and have greater disease resistance than onions or garlic, which makes them popular with many growers. They need to be grown from seed, either in modules or in open ground and transplanted to a permanent growing site when large enough. Leeks are a good follow-on crop after new potatoes, spring cabbages or a green manure such as mustard or clover. They prefer a fertile, well-drained soil, will tolerate some shade and remain in good condition for many months, so can be harvested throughout the winter. You can grow a lot of leeks in a small space!

Sow leeks indoors in modules for early crops in February–March, or outdoors in a seedbed from March to April. If using modules, allow four seeds per large cell and plant out as a block, allowing 8–10in (20–25cm) between blocks. Keep seedlings weed-free and watered to encourage steady growth.

Leeks are said to be ready to transplant when as thick as a pencil, but will manage to make fair-sized plants at much less than this – they'll just take a while longer to get there. Planting leeks is very satisfying and a good job for primary school aged kids – make a hole with a dibber about 6in (15cm) deep, repeat every 6–10in (15–25cm) and drop a leek plant down each hole. Using a watering can without a rose, fill the hole with water and the job's done. Harvest from anytime that they're big enough to eat.

Beans – Broad, Runner and French

Broad beans are the hardiest and first to crop of all the bean family. In mild well-drained areas, they can be sown in November to crop in early June, but for most of the country a reliable crop can be first sown outside in March. Alternatively seeds can be sown in rolled-up newspaper tubes, trays or 3in (9cm) pots indoors and transplanted to speed things up – this is a particularly useful technique if you live somewhere with a healthy rodent or bird population, which love eating bean seeds. Broad beans, especially the shorter cultivars such as 'The Sutton', perform well in containers, and are very good for roof gardens, because they're wind-tolerant.

Sow seeds in a zigzag double row outside, allowing 3–6in (6–15cm) between plants and 24–36in between the rows depending on the height of the cultivar. Tall growing plants will need stakes and string to support them as the pods develop. Harvest as soon as you can feel the beans through the pods.

Runner beans seem such an English plant it's hard to realize they originally came from South America, except in those chilly summers when the flowers refuse to set, because the plants, like their growers, would sooner be somewhere warmer! Once they've started to set, runner beans are one of the most productive of all vegetable crops. Expect anything up to 35lb (16kg) of beans from a 10ft (3m) row.

Plant runner beans in pots for very early crops, usually 2–3 weeks before the last frost is likely, or directly into the soil a little later. Traditionally runner beans are planted up a double row of canes, or a wigwam structure, but almost any sort of support will do, provided it's solid enough to take the weight of full-grown plants thrashing around in a late summer gale. Textbooks recommend sowing two seeds per cane, but I usually like to sow double this, to allow for damage by slugs. Alternatively growing runner beans in borders alongside other flowering plants is a good way of displaying their beautiful red, white or pink flowers.

When harvesting, older runner beans which have become too stringy for eating can be shelled and simmered to make splendid soups or bean stews, but remember they must be boiled hard for ten minutes (like dried kidney beans) to destroy any toxins.

French beans are sometimes called string beans, kidney beans or haricot beans, and are as easy to grow as runners, but often perform better in containers. In some conditions they are more ready to set pods.

Like runners, they need warm soil to grow in and shouldn't be sown outdoors before late April even in mild areas. There are dwarf and climbing varieties of French bean – you get higher crops from the same area of ground from climbing types, but the dwarf cultivars are quicker to crop.

French beans can be eaten as shelled dried beans as well as the more normal fresh, so if you get a glut leave some beans to dry on the plants – it's usually easier to do this on climbing varieties, as there's better air circulation. Certain cultivars

Broad beans 'Aquadulce Claudia', the hardiest type for overwintering.

Borlotto beans drying for winter use.

Sticked peas.

are better for dry beans than fresh, including 'Horsehead' and 'Triomph de Farcy'. Leave beans on the plants until the pods are papery textured, then pick and shell them. Dry the shelled beans on a tray before storing them in sealed jars or bags. Of course, if you haven't eaten them all by spring, you can always plant them next year.

Peas

Peas are an extravagant crop for a smaller garden, and in dry soils or sites are a waste of space unless they have plenty of extra water, but the taste of really fresh peas makes up for all of these disadvantages. Every child surely deserves that time-consuming job of pea-podding with the chance to eat most before they reach the saucepan.

The taller varieties of pea take up less space if grown as a pyramid or wall-mounted crop rather than a row. The coloured flowered types, such as mangetout 'Carouby de Mausanne', which can reach 6ft (2m) tall with brilliant pink and purple flowers, look marvellously ornamental.

Peas can be sown in late October to mid November in well-drained soils just like broad beans, but these sowings will need to be the hardier round-seeded cultivars. Make a second sowing in February under cover or outside in March. Mice are partial to peas, so try to protect early sowings with fleece or prickly twigs scattered along the rows. Later sowings in April can be of the wrinkle seeded, sweeter types. If you are troubled by sparrows pecking at the young plants protect them by using bottle cloches or try growing some of the semi-leafless cultivars such as 'Markana' which having very thin, wiry foliage look already chewed, encouraging the birds to leave them alone. Once the plants have reached a few inches tall their attraction for birds seems to vanish. Last sowings, just after midsummer, should be mangetout or sugar snaps which mature quickly.

Plant peas about 4in (10cm) apart in a double row, or two plants every 6in (15cm) in a pyramid: if growing from seed add a few more at the ends of the row to make up for any gaps. All peas need support: pea sticks, stakes or bamboos with twine or netting.

Expect at least four good servings of peas from a short row of 5ft (1.8m) long, more from the taller cultivars, and over six servings from mangetout or sugar snap. The immature sprouts will add flavour to stir-fries and soups, while the nitrogen-fixing roots enhance soil fertility.

Peas succeed in containers when given a good depth of soil to help them stay upright: old cooking oil drums are excellent, as are windowbox-style wooden packing crates.

Courgettes, Squashes, Pumpkins and Marrows

A courgette has to be 12in (30cm) long before it becomes a fully fledged marrow, but if you pick fruits before this a plant can produce fruit continually from July through to September. Unless you are particularly dedicated to Mediterranean cookery you will only need one plant per person. A courgette or bush marrow can be kept within the area of a single square yard/metre, or trained upwards on a strong support which will need tying in regularly.

Winter squashes develop a thick hard skin enabling them to keep over several months. One plant will only grow a single huge pumpkin or about four large ones, and cover about double the space of a marrow.

All the marrow family are happy growing in large, preferably very large – at least 10–12in (25–30cm) deep – containers, provided you water them well and regularly. They can be really productive in a potted courtyard garden, where the large leaves make a tropical effect.

Sow two seeds per large module or 3in (9cm) pot, sowing indoors in late April to May depending on the date of the usual last frosts in your area, and discard the weaker seedling if both emerge. Grow on until at least three true leaves have formed before beginning to harden off and plant out once

Growing annual chrysanthemums close to this courgette will encourage beneficial insects, which eat pests such as greenfly.

conditions are warm enough at least 4ft (1.3m) apart. All the members of the Cucurbitaceae are slug magnets, so protect your plants with all means possible – nematodes, bran or bottle cloches – until established.

Cabbages, Kale and Sprouting Broccoli

The cabbage family is vast, but almost all require the same conditions – fertile alkaline soil, plenty of space around them, good light, adequate drainage and firm roots. Most are fine for a smaller vegetable garden, except swedes or Brussels sprouts, and a few are tolerant of large pots.

Brassicas take up a large area for a long time – sometimes from one spring to the next – but are very hardy and will compensate for their long growing season by having an equally lengthy harvesting period. For gardeners with limited space, a few plants of kale or spring greens are better than the fussier subjects such as cauliflowers. Some, especially the purple-leaved types, are very decorative edible ornamentals.

Brassicas require fertile soil with a pH of 7.5 to 8. Don't overfeed plants which are to overwinter, because of the danger of frost damage, especially if cold weather follows a prolonged mild spell.

They are a good successor to a green manure such as field beans or a follow-on crop from a previously manured crop, e.g. potatoes or cucurbits. It's often recommended to follow a brassica crop with onions, as the exudates from onion roots destroy or repel some of the root disorders of brassicas.

Two of the biggest problems with growing brassicas are winged pests – caterpillars and pigeons. The only surefire way of protecting against both

Cabbage and kale are ornamental edibles in the right place.

of these is netting – you may decide to construct a walk-in structure similar to a fruit cage, or support a smaller cover on poles. Female cabbage white butterflies have an irritating habit of squeezing their backsides through netting in order to drop eggs on plants beneath, so either make the netting cover taller than you expect the plants to grow or use very fine gauge netting (Enviromesh). Cutleafed kale e.g. 'Hungry Gap' and 'Red Russian', are more resistant to bird damage as it looks already eaten from a pigeon's-eye view.

Sowing brassicas in modules reduces the risk of clubroot.

Sow *sprouting broccoli* and *kale* in open ground or in modules, from April to May and thin out to give healthy uncrowded plants before transplanting in June to July. If *calabrese* is rather more exacting as it resents root disturbance, so use biodegradable pots or sow in pinches and thin to a single seedling.

When transplanting seedlings, bury the root and lower stem deeply to avoid damage by cabbage rootfly; stamp around the seedlings to give a firm rooting area. Kale and sprouting broccoli will require at least 3ft (1m) between plants if grown in rows for maximum development, but you can plant at 2ft (60cm) apart in blocks. Calabrese will produce smaller heads all at once if grown close together, bigger heads over a longer period if spaced wider apart.

Cabbage can be grown all year round, from overwintering cultivars such as 'Flower of Spring' and 'Cotswold Queen', sown in autumn to harvest early spring, through early summer cultivars sown in March to mature a few months later, e.g. 'Greyhound' or 'Derby Day', then high temperature-resistant summer to autumn cultivars like 'Minicole' and 'Winningstadt', followed by the very hardy, stronger tasting 'Celtic' or 'January King' which will last all winter.

Sow in modules or a seedbed and space transplants or thinnings anything from 12 to 20in (30–50 cm) apart depending on the time they are

to crop, with winter harvesting plants having the widest spacing. Planting distance affects the size of cabbage: spring greens can be harvested at as close as 4in (10cm) apart, but if you remove every other plant as soon as they reach eating size, the remainder can produce small-hearted spring cabbages later.

Alternatively you can simply plant a quick crop of spring greens at any time of year whenever there's space in the garden, except during the depths of winter, rather than waiting for a true headed cabbage. Choose a quick maturing cultivar such as 'Hispi', and sow in pinches 10–15in (25–35cm) apart, then either eat along the row or take out alternate plants.

Turnips and *kohl rabi* are a useful summer catch crop, being ready in as little as six to eight weeks from sowing. Sow in small pinches 6in (15cm) apart, and keep well-watered for tender tasty roots.

Salads and Leafy Vegetables

Lettuce can be sown and harvested almost all year round. Other salad vegetables are equally if not even more versatile. You should be able to provide year round fresh leafy supplies from a very limited space. They need a fairly fertile soil, a reasonably sunny site and plenty of water in warm weather to keep the leaves tender.

Lettuce can be sown thickly, to snip with scissors when a few inches high (cut-and-come again), thinned selectively or transplanted to wider spacings for full sized heads. Curly, looseleaf cultivars of lettuces don't form a true heart and so can be picked over a long period without losing quality. Some are quite cold-hardy. Butterhead and crisphead (iceberg) varieties need warmer temperatures,

but the cos types are the most winter hardy. Sow as late as the end of September in favoured gardens to grow on slowly through the winter.

During very hot weather lettuce seeds often won't germinate, but this heat-induced dormancy is readily reversible as soon as the weather cools down. Soaking drills with very cold water late in the evening may help. A more environmentally sound stratagem is to grow a different plant which is more suited to the season. Simply scatter seed in any sunny spare area of soil every couple of weeks during the growing season for an endless supply of young leaves.

Heat tolerant leafy vegetables for eating young include frisee or curly leafed *endive*; the slightly bitter tasting *chervil* and seedling *Florence fennel*, both with fine aniseed flavoured leaves looking rather like carrot tops; *corn salad*, *beetroot* and *mizuna* from May sowings; *nasturtium* leaves; baby *spinach*; as well as seedling *chicory* and coriander.

Cold tolerant leaf vegetables include members of the cabbage family, such as *rocket*, and *American* or *land cress*, both extremely fast to germinate; the oriental *mustard greens* and *pak chois* together with *mizuna*; *corn salad*, *chervil* and *coriander* again from late August to September sowings; *Claytonia* or *miner's lettuce* which is high in vitamin C, and all the different types of overwintering *hearting chicories* including *radicchio*.

If you have a cold frame or even a well-lit shed, mixed salads can be sown in deep boxes from February through late March and again from August through to October, to cut during the colder months of the year. Salads are probably the easiest of all the crops you can cultivate, even if you haven't got a garden.

Carrots, Parsnips and Beetroots

Beetroot is relatively easy to grow, needing a fertile but not over-rich soil, deep enough to retain moisture at the right time. Carrots and parsnips are slightly more challenging, needing a light, stone-free soil – if you garden on very rocky land, deep clay or a thin shallow soil over chalk they may not be your first choice. Both carrots and parsnips need a well-drained soil which has not been recently manured, which will cause them to

Chicory 'Precoce de Treviso' tastes as good as it looks.

Parsnips growing with shallow-rooted annual scarlet flax, Linum grandiflorum rubrum, *to confuse carrot root fly.*

grow 'fangy' with lots of divided roots instead of a single smooth one. Try to sow thinly, to avoid disturbance by thinning, as this limits the damage done by rootfly.

Parsnips are often difficult to germinate, often requiring a cool period to break seed dormancy. As the seed deteriorates rapidly with age, always buy fresh seed each year: I find it helps to have seed from several different suppliers as well, as some years germination can be extremely erratic. They are not really suitable for growing in containers, unless you use drainpipes or two pieces of guttering held together with cable-ties, as keen exhibitors do for flower shows, to achieve the ultimate long white roots. They have a long growing season but can be harvested all winter.

Sow parsnips thinly whenever the soil is workable from late February to April. The seed is very light, so keep your hand close to the ground when sowing or it can blow away. Grown in a bed system or as a staggered double row in a shallow drill about 8in (20cm) wide, they can be sown in pinches about 6in (15cm) apart.

Parsnip seed can be mixed with radishes so you can see where you sowed them, because they germinate slowly – up to six weeks – but pulling the radishes up often damages the seedling parsnips, so I prefer to sow a little cos lettuce instead, which can be cut off and eaten as seedling salad without damaging fragile roots.

Apart from removing weeds, leave undisturbed until large enough to harvest. Mulching with a thin layer of grass-cuttings can deter carrot rootfly.

Carrots need warmer conditions to germinate in and shouldn't be sown until March at the earliest. They can be sown throughout the summer until early August. Avoid sowing carrots immediately after digging in a green manure, as the seeds are small and may not grow.

Rhubarb chard is a very decorative edible crop and looks as well in a flower border as it does in the vegetable patch.

Station sowing in a bed is probably the best method, or a single row between other crops to deter the dreaded carrot rootfly. If sowing in a bed allow 4–6in (10–15cm) between every pinch of three to five seeds. In a single row space seeds a little closer, every 4in (10cm) for medium sized or early cropping roots, to double that to produce the largest maincrop harvest. Young carrots can be pulled in late July from a March sowing, or left to fully develop by autumn.

Carrots are liable to split in dry weather if left unwatered.

There are a number of carrot cultivars which are claimed to be less prone to rootfly damage than others, but I've personally found they taste far less attractive than conventional types.

Beetroot seed is normally a multiple container, with a cluster of seed within the lumpy exterior, so sow them at 6–9in (15–22cm) intervals in a block or bed and thin out individual clusters to one or two seedlings, unless you want baby beets. (Beet seedling leaves can be used in salads.) A few selected cultivars are monogerm (only have one seedling develop per seed), e.g. 'Solo'.

The seed can be sown in modules in late February or directly into the soil from March to late June. When planting out modules space them at 8in (20cm) apart. Irrigate during dry spells to prevent roots becoming tough and woody. Harvest as soon as the roots are big enough: twist off the leaves to reduce bleeding, rather than cutting them.

Beetroot grow well in containers. They tolerate a little shade, as well as salt, which is useful if you garden by the coast or close to a busy road. They are damaged by hard frosts or heavy rains, so store inside or process them before winter.

Beetroot can be white, yellow or striped as well as the ordinary red, and can be round or cylindrical in shape.

CHAPTER 7

Specific sites and awkward spots

WHAT'S YOUR MICROCLIMATE?

Any garden, even the smallest, already has a number of climate zones within it – there probably will be a shady or at least damper patch, a sunny warm spot or two, a windy place and a more sheltered corner. By recognizing what your garden is capable of growing, you can adapt it to the sort of planting scheme you need.

To establish which way your garden faces, find out where the sun rises and sets. Look at neighbouring buildings to see if they are liable to cast a shade during the winter months when the sun is lowest. South-west facing plots will always be warmer than north-east aspects. Remember, exposure to frost and winds is more dependent on the aspect of the garden than on its latitude: you may be surprised by what will survive!

Sometimes a garden can be colder than expected, and this may be due to it being situated in a frost prone area. Frost pockets are caused by cold air (which is heavier than warm) rolling downhill until it fills a low valley, or is sometimes blocked by a building, hedge or wall preventing the passage of air downhill. In such places making a hole in a wall in the lowest part of the site, if possible, can have dramatic benefits, although it may not make you popular with the owners of gardens below.

Is your plot next to a large expanse of brickwork, which will act as a storage heater? Or is it on the edge of a windy hill with only a low wall or half-grown hedge for shelter? Hedges filter the wind, while walls can funnel it, so beware of wind tunnel effects, particularly among new housing developments where trees and shrubs have yet to establish, or amongst tall buildings.

Gardens in cities are often a few degrees warmer

Cold ivy berries rimmed in hoar frost.

than the surrounding countryside. Plants here will have to cope with lower light levels due to pollution, and less rainfall – and what falls may be more acidic, high in particulates and gritty from constant movement of heavy traffic. Pools of deep shade receive blast furnace heat reflected from other buildings, rather than becoming cooler when out of the sun.

What you grow will depend partly on where you live, as well as your personal preferences. In the sheltered South West counties there will be a wider range of species available to cultivation than in the North East or even the Midlands. Growers in the southern part of the UK will find that not only is their insect population more varied than those in the North, because of the warmer climate, but they're more likely to have exotic immigrants flying or being blown over the Channel.

Large trees will give some shelter from the worst weather and filter polluted air from nearby roads,

The easiest way to find a really warm spot in your garden is to study what's already in residence! Cats sleep in a tight curl up to 45°F, and a half-curl up to 65°F... after which they tend to look for shade.

but trees often rob nutrients and water from your soil in summer. A nearby ditch or stream may mean you have to think about the possibility of part of your garden being underwater from time to time, particularly if your house is in a low lying area – or the house may even be flooded.

It's well worth asking the neighbours what extreme weather conditions have happened in the past, as well as seeing what plants look happiest in established gardens close by.

Gardens by the coast usually suffer less from frosts than other areas, but will be scorched by strong salt- and sand-laden winds, attacking tender leaves with chemical and mechanical effects. Similar damage can be caused if your garden is sited next to a quarry, industrial site or busy motorway, as airborne debris strips layers from a plant's sensitive epidermis. Only the armour-plated can survive.

KNOW YOUR SOIL

From a distance the difference between mud, earth or soil can only be seen in colour– but get a little closer and the different types are quite distinctive. To find out what your soil's really like, treat it like the true friend it can be and gently caress a handful – and just as you would for a lover, handle it without gloves. When you rub a little between your fingers, does it feel smooth and silky, rough and gritty or somewhere in between?

Clays are heavy, sticky when wet and pliable – if rubbed between the fingers they feel smooth, like expensive soap. In the garden they are hard work, becoming very difficult to dig when wet and often leaving water standing in ruts or hollows: sometimes if the water lies long in them, the earth turns strange colours and becomes blue or grey. When clays dry out, they set concrete hard and split open into deep cracks. Clay soils are cold, and warm up slowly in spring. Against this unwelcoming exterior, clays are very fertile and the most productive of all soil types.

Sands are dramatically different, feeling light in the hand and easily crumbling to trickle through the fingers. They feel gritty and rough. Sandy soils are easy to work in the garden, heating up quickly

and draining so that even after days of heavy rain it's still possible to dig almost as soon as the rain stops. When dry enough sands can even blow away in strong winds. Sandy soils are hungry and thirsty – they dry quickly to a dust, and however much organic matter is added, it quickly vanishes without much long-lasting effect.

Silts have a mixture of the qualities of a sand and a clay, but have a few extra ones of their own – they are reasonably fertile, are not too hard to work, drain relatively well and rarely waterlog, but often form a hard surface layer or cap when finely cultivated, especially once rain falls. This can make for problems when growing fine leaved plants from seed, such as carrots, which haven't the power to penetrate the soil in this state.

Loams are the happy medium between clays, silts and sands, having the best parts of each. A good loam should form a ball when a handful is squeezed, which crumbles when lightly tapped. Loamy soils work easily, drain well but retain moisture and have rich depths of nutrients for plants to draw on.

All soils are affected by the drainage of their surrounding areas: even sands can become water-logged in certain situations. On very wet sites, the amount of groundwater can become a problem, as the soil tends to swell with excess water and distort foundations of paths or walls.

Spotted orchids growing wild on chalk grassland in the Peak District.

Figwort always grows in damp places.

For wildflowers, each soil has its native type of flora and associated wildlife. The highest density of species is found not, as you might imagine, on the richest soils but on the poorest, mostly alkaline sandy soils of chalk downland. To create a truly diverse wildflower meadow you need an impoverished soil, and if all you have is a former vegetable plot it's probably better to think again and grow greedier herbaceous plants or shrubs instead.

Looking at what's growing already can give a clue to what conditions may be like below. An old farmer's saying is that a good soil will grow big fat weeds, so if you have only a few stunted starved weeds, you might be justified in feeling worried. Chickweed and nettles indicate plentiful nitrogen supplies, while clovers thrive in nitrogen deficient soils. Docks and creeping buttercups thrive on heavy land, while scentless mayweed, spurreys, sun spurge or hawkbits all need lighter, sandier conditions. Figwort, lamb's quarters or chenopodiums and *Persicaria* species show up most on damp rich soil, sheep's sorrel and wild pansy indicate a low pH, while wild carrot and meadow cranesbill show alkalinity.

Probably the best way of finding out more about your soil is to dig a hole – or several, if you feel energetic enough. You don't have to dig a new version of the Channel Tunnel, just excavate a cube at least two spade depths deep, which is as far as most plant roots will reach.

As you dig, consider what you find – is the soil very hard, or full of stones, or worse, old bricks and lumps of concrete? If the plot is part of a new build you may discover a thin layer of good, often imported, topsoil over a heavily compacted layer of builder's rubble, rammed earth and poor quality material which doesn't resemble anything you're likely to desire in a garden.

On older houses your excavations can uncover all sorts of foundations – anything from defunct air-raid shelters and former greenhouse or shed bases with their attendant broken glass and old metal, to possibly even old wells or privies. Soils around older properties may sometimes have a heavily compacted layer about a spade deep, where cultivation has been limited to areas above – this hard, sometimes almost impenetrable layer is called a *pan*, and will need breaking by deeper cultivation, usually with a crowbar, if you want to grow vegetables or fruit well.

If you are lucky, your soil will be none of these, and if you are very fortunate, you may inherit a deep, stone-free, black crumbling loam, rich in many years' fertility. If you do, please cherish it as a genuine heirloom and treasure!

Having dug your hole, pour a bucket of water into it and watch how quickly it drains away – or doesn't, in some cases. For best results, try to carry out this test in dry conditions, as if there's been a lot of rain it won't be so easy to see any difference.

Greater chickweed is an indicator of high nitrogen levels in the soil.

If there's water in the bottom of your hole already when it hasn't been raining recently, is there a problem with drainage? Or are you digging in a hollow?

If there is a particular patch in the garden which is permanently damp and you don't live at the bottom of a hill, there may be a spring or underground water beneath. On many soils these damp patches are very seasonal, being caused by pockets of hidden clay below a well-draining topsoil which temporarily retain water, so the water only flows in the winter or early spring. These are often nonpermanent features, persisting for a few seasons before being broken up by the action of worms or plant roots. Banging a long metal pole into the damp soil can also improve drainage, but ideally you need to take more drastic action. Dig a big deep trench until you hit the water table – which sometimes is a lot closer than you think – and fill the lower 6–10 inches with hardcore, then top up with the soil so you end up with a ridge about 6in above the original soil level. A lot depends on how wet your boggy patch is, what you are trying to grow (really, if it's that awkward the ecological answer is don't grow anything that doesn't want to be there) and how much time/energy/ hardcore

Native sea-kale, Crambe maritima, *and sea pea,* Lathyrus maritima, *growing within splash-reach of the highest tide.*

Centranthus rubor, also known as red valerian delights in dry stony places. It can rapidly become invasive in a garden.

you've got. Damp areas can form attractive features such as raingardens, temporary ponds and bog plantings.

COASTAL GARDENS – SALT AND WINDS

Rarely freezing, gardens by the sea are hard places for anything with tender leaves to live, so select plants which can stand desiccation and tolerate salt. Next time you travel along a major road in April, look at the verge nearest the kerbside for the low growing tufts of white flowers which mark the salt-tolerant scurvy cress, growing commonly inland wherever road salt is spread. Plants have to be very tough to do well in the extremes of a salt-laden soil and tend to become ruthlessly invasive in gentler sites, so be warned – keep a hoe handy to repel over-enthusiastic species.

Many annuals do well in salty soils, and a good example is the UK native, viper's bugloss, *Echium vulgare* and its garden relatives. It thrives on gravel, and although fairly short-lived will set seed freely, so you only ever need to buy one packet of seeds. The individual flowers are small but there are plenty of them constantly throughout the summer, visited by bees and predatory insects. Other good choices for a seaside garden include: hollyhocks and other mallows, whose young leaves and flowers can be eaten in salads or cooked as a spinach substitute; the deliciously scented biennial wallflowers; all types of stock (*Mattiola*); and Iceland poppies with deceptively fragile bright petals in early summer.

SEASIDE INLAND

Garden plants which tolerate both road and sea salt include:

Shrubs
Arbutus unedo
Artemesia spp
Atriplex canescens
Caryopteris (all, except golden leaved forms)
Cotoneaster spp
Cytissus spp
Elaeagnus x ebbingii, E. pungens & E. umbellata
Escallonia (all green leaved forms)
Euphorbia
Fuchsia magellanica
Genista spp
Helianthemum
Hippophae rhamnoides
Hebe spp
Lupinus arboreus
Malva spp
Rosmarinus officinalis
Tamarisk

Herbaceous Perennials
Althaea spp
Corydalis lutea
Cotyledon vulgarae
Erodium
Eryngium
Erysimum
Lupinus
Lathyrus maritimus
Lavandula
Levisticum
Limonum
Marrubium vulgare
Papaver
Silene

Annuals and Biennials
Cheiranthus cheri & C. alloniii
Eschscholzia
Hesperis matronalis
Matthiola

Grasses
Ammophila breviligulata, A. arenaria
Chasmanthium latifolium
Leymus arenarius
Spartinum pectina 'Aureomarginata'

Vegetables
Almost all of the cabbage family (but Brussels sprouts may not tolerate coastal gales without 'blowing' or bolting)
Asparagus
Beetroot
Horseradish
Leaf beet
Purslane
Sorrel
Spinach
Seakale

Fruit
Rhubarb
Sweet chestnuts (these are surprisingly salt tolerant, if rather large for most gardens)

ANALYSING CONDITIONS – ACID OR ALKALINE?

What is the pH of Your Soil?

The pH scale is a 14-point measure of the free hydrogen ions in the soil, but without longwinded scientific explanations, all gardeners need to know is that neutral is 7, acid is below and alkaline is above. Acidity or alkalinity of a soil is one of the most important factors influencing the plants which will or won't grow on it. Some, such as rhododendrons, are acid loving (calcifuges) and others require alkaline conditions, often called lime-lovers or calciphiles. The levels of minerals available for plants increase (sometimes to toxic amounts) or lessen as pH changes. Most vegetables are happiest with a slightly acidic soil, pH around 6.5, but can cope with levels greater or lower than this without too many problems.

Acidic soils are those which have a pH of less than 7 (in the UK it is rare to encounter anything lower than 4.5, about the same acidity as lemon juice).

Alkaline soils have a pH between 7.1 and 8.8 or so. Higher alkalinity is also rare in the UK, although it can be encountered in former industrial sites or in desert conditions.

To determine the soil pH, get a simple test kit which can be bought from garden centres. It uses a liquid indicator which changes colour when in contact with soil dissolved in de-ionized water. (De-ionized water is sold for topping-up car batteries or steam irons.) If you don't have a kit handy, study the neighbours' gardens – if the hydrangeas are pink flowered, you can't see a single rhododendron, skimmia or azalea which isn't growing in a pot but there are plenty of pinks, carnations, hardy geraniums and irises, you are probably on an alkaline soil. On the other hand, if the place heaves with heathers, camellias and rhododendrons, while the hydrangeas have blue flowers, it's most likely acidic soil.

Very acidic soils frequently occur in areas of high rainfall, so are often wet for most of the year with a high proportion of organic matter, usually present as peat. Bear in mind the nature of the soil as well as its pH: an alkaline clay will support a population of plants very different from a well-drained limestone soil.

ABOVE: *Rhodedendrons and azaleas are calcifuges, i.e. they cannot tolerate limestone soil.*

BELOW: *The leaves of this* Fothergilla gardenii *'Blue Shadow' are just beginning to develop their magnificent autumn colour.*

For a sheltered site on dampish, slightly acidic soil *Fothergilla gardenii* 'Blue Shadow' has scented spikes of feathery blooms in May, but its true glory is the uniquely blue-grey foliage colour reminiscent of a blue hosta or an exotic cabbage, with a heavy greyish bloom. In autumn the leaves become brilliant flame-red and shades of orange.

Plants for Acid Soils

Plants marked # will tolerate dry conditions

Trees and Shrubs

Acer cissifolium
Azalea
Calluna vulgaris
Cassiope
Cercis siliquastrum
Clethra alnifolia
Colutea arborescens #
Erica #
Genista #
Hibiscus #
Helianthemum #
Indigofera #
Kalmia
Lithodora diffusa
Lonicera #
Pernyetta mucronata
Rhododendron
Vaccinium (all)
Viburnum opulus

Herbaceous plants

Astilbe
Arum #
Dodecatheon
Gentiana
Jasione
Lobelia cardinalis
Meconopsis
Rogersia
Primula
Saxifraga fortunei
Tiarella

Grasses

Deschampsia flexuosa
Festuca (all)
Melica uniflora
Molina (all)

Vegetables

Beetroot
Broad beans
Leaf beet
Leeks
Onions
Potatoes
Sorrel
Spinach

Fruit

For truly acid soils: blueberries and cranberries
For moderate acidity: blackcurrants, raspberries, gooseberries and rhubarb

Plants for Alkaline Soils

Trees and shrubs

Acer campestre, A. ginnala or A. circinatum, A. glabrum, A. nikoense (all of which should be planted more than they are)
Carpinus betulus
Cercis siliquastrum
Ceanothus
Daphne
Deutzia
Eleagnus
Hebe
Lonicera
Morus nigra
Phillyrea
Rosmarinus
Sorbus aria
Syringa
Thymus

Herbaceous Plants

Aster oblongifolius
*Calamintha cretica, C. nepeta (*syn *Acinos alpinus)*
Cirsium echinocephalum, C. japonicum
Dianthus (all)
Dipsascus
Echium
Erigeron
Erodium
Galactites
Geranium
Origanum laevigatum (and relatives)
Salvia forskaohlei, S. officinalis, S. nemorosa
Saxifraga longifolia (most mossy types and all silver forms)
Scabiosa (all)
Silybum marianum
Verbascum

Grasses

Briza maxima, B. media
Calamagrostis varia
Carex montana
Koeleria glauca
Sesleria caerulea

Vegetables

Brassicas (all)
Chicory
Florence fennel
French and runner beans
Globe and Jerusalem artichokes
Lettuce
Onions
Parsnips
Salsify and scorzonera
Sweetcorn
Tomatoes

Galactites tomentosa is an attractive, if prickly, plant that is happiest growing on hot shallow soils over chalk or limestone.

Fruit

Stone fruit (all)
Gooseberries
Raspberries (if fed with a seaweed extract or with chelated iron)
Rhubarb

SHADE

Shade can be cast from buildings, fencing or trees, and of these possibilities large trees, such as beech, are perhaps the most challenging, because they not only shade plants but are much greedier competitors for water and nutrients. Evergreen trees or a building casting permanent shade are more difficult to deal with than deciduous trees, where early flowering bulbs can bloom before the leaves have spread.

Possibly the worst-case scenario is a combination of a tall building coupled with a *Chamaecyparissus x leylandii* hedge occupying the south and west of a site.

A large number of plants will tolerate shade, particularly if there is an adequate water supply, but the choice may be somewhat limited, and the garden's main display may peak early in the year. Ponds in particular need at least half a day of sunlight daily, and to grow any sort of vegetables requires at least four to five hours of direct sunlight daily.

Candelabra primroses make a delightful underplanting on a damp acid soil.

Pieris forestii is a good choice for acidic soils that don't dry out completely.

Try to incorporate as much organic matter as you can into the soil to aid moisture retention, and mulch heavily to retain soil moisture. Boost reflected light levels by painting walls or fences white, laying white plastic on the ground between the plants and using pale paving if possible. For those who find expense is no object, micro-irrigation piping will enable a wide range of vegetation to flourish in even the most difficult conditions. Damp shade, natural or artificial, will give a wider selection of plants which will survive.

Shade Tolerant Plants

Trees and shrubs

Actaea spicata
Buxus sempervirens
Daphne laureola, D. mezereum
Epimedium
x fatshedera lizei
Fatsia japonica
Prunus lusitanica
Rubus odoratus, R. spectabilis
Sarcococca
Skimmia
Vinca

SHADE TOLERANT EDIBLE PLANTS

(* will survive in very wet but not waterlogged sites
better for drier shade)

Vegetables
Beetroot
Cabbage family (except Brussels sprouts or cauli-flower)
Cucumber *
Hamburg parsley *
Leek *
Onion sets (autumn sown)
Peas (sown late)
Salads: corn salad *, landcress *, cut-and-come-again lettuce, endive # (spring sowings), oriental greens #, sorrel *
Swiss chard #, spinach *, perpetual spinach #
Turnip (to overwinter)

Fruit
Raspberries, wild strawberries and rhubarb are the most shade-tolerant of the fruit crops, and will do quite well providing they have at least four hours of sunlight during the day, although they tolerate shade from buildings far better than being under a large tree. They all need summer moisture, disliking a dry root run during the fruiting season as much as being flooded in winter.

Herbaceous plants

Anemone
Ajuga
Arum
Astilbe
Astrantia
Brunnera
Erythronium
Digitalis
Geranium nodosum, G. sylvaticum
Helleborus foetidus, H. x hybridus
Heuchera
Iris foetidissimum
Mentha piperata, M. spicata, M. citrata
Primula (most)
Ranunculus aconitifolius
Rheum palmatum
Saxifraga fortuneii (and most mossy saxifrages)
Tiarella
Viola

Grasses

Brachypodium sylvaticum
Bromus racemosus
Carex (all)

SUN

Sunny gardens are often dry as well as being exposed to strong winds. High soil temperatures

ABOVE: *Climbing plants that need good drainage can make the best use of a sunny wall, like this* Wisteria sinensis.

BELOW: Clerodendrum trichotomum *has powerfully scented flowers in late summer*

near the surface can inhibit worm action, as well as shrivel roots in the top layers, leading to capping of soil and run-off when rain falls.

A striking plant for sunny gardens favoured by garden designers is the cardoon, *Cynara carduncu-lus,* a gigantic thistle whose stems were once considered edible. A single plant will take lots of room – up to a square yard/metre as a minimum – and flowers mostly during July and August, feeding bumble and hive bees alike. The flamboyant flowerheads can be removed once the brilliant blue petals have faded, or they can be left to make huge dramatic silhouettes on frosty mornings, when the old stems will award safe harbour for beneficial insects such as anthracoid bugs, lacewings and others over the winter.

A sunny spot against a wall makes for extra winter protection, provided it isn't facing due east: try growing the beautiful *Clerodendrum trichotomum* here: possibly the best cultivar is var. *fargesii* AGM. Beautifully scented flowers, fragranced like concentrated jasmine and honeysuckle in late summer, are followed by persistent turquoise blue berries in crimson calyxes. This simply must not have a place that's too hot or dry. Other plants which benefit from the shelter of a wall in the cooler areas of the country include kiwi fruits, which swarm merrily to over 12ft (4m) in a summer, or the much shorter semi-shrubby plume poppy, *Romneya coulteri,* with snow white flowers and smooth glaucous foliage.

Many plants tolerant of dry sunny conditions have silver or grey leaves which reflect light, or small leaves to minimize desiccation.

Sun Tolerant Plants

Trees and Shrubs

Abelia chinesis, A. triflora
Cytissus
Fuchsia
Genista
Lavendula
Lupinus arboreus
Prostanthera
Romneya coulteri
Rosmarinus officinalis
Salvia

Herbaceous Plants

Alcea rosea and related species (hollyhock)
Artemisia
Asclepsis syriaca and *A. tuberosa*
Centranthus rubor
Cerinthe major
Coreopsis
Dictamus albus
Erodium pelargoniifolium
Eryngium (all)
Euphorbia (all)
Gallardia
Hyssopus officinalis
Liatris (all)
Marrubium vulgare
Monarda fistulosa
Nepeta (all)
Papaver (all)
*Phlomis samia, P. tuberosa, P. viscosa (*syn *P. russeliana)*
Polemonium
Sedum telephium, S. superbum
Sempervivum (houseleek*)*
Sisyrinchium
Silybum marianum
Tithonia

Grasses

Achantherum calamagrostis
Andropogon gerardii
Elymus hispidus, E. magellanicus
Festuca glauca
Pennisetum alopecuroides
Stipa gigantea
Ucinina rubra

Fruit

Peaches
Grapes
Figs
Strawberries

Vegetables

Most vegetables tolerate sunny, dry conditions if allowed to establish with irrigation first. Leafy greens tend to do better than those which form pods or tubers.

Amaranthus (calaloo)
Cos lettuce
Dwarf French and soya beans
New Zealand spinach
Pumpkins
Purslane
Sweetcorn
Tomatoes

Herbs and flowers: Almost all herbs and most hardy annual flowers relish a sunny site, preferably with an impoverished soil.

EXPOSURE

Large trees will give some shelter from the worst weather and filter polluted air from nearby roads, but these often rob nutrients and water from your soil in summer. When planting shrubs or small trees, try to site the taller species nearest the windiest side of your plot, so as to filter the worst winds.

London Pride, Saxifraga umbrosa, *growing through a golden prostrate juniper – a pleasing selection for a semi-shaded border.*

*Yew (*Taxus baccata*) berries are relished by birds.*

You may need to erect artificial screens or wind barriers until the plants making up your wind-break have had a chance to grow away. Plastic and rubber windbreak materials look unsightly but work well for a few years to give shrubs a chance: the plastic materials can be recycled, or in moderately exposed areas brushwood or hurdles provide temporary shelter which is biodegradable.

Roof gardeners will find that plants dry out far more rapidly than those on ground level, and may be unable to use containers as large as they want, due to weight. Here micro-irrigation really comes into its own, but make sure that the pipes are secured well between plants: wind speeds a few stories up are violent and often inconsistent in direction. Grasses are ideal to filter winds on the boundaries of a roof garden, particularly the tougher species such as *Miscanthus sinensis* or *Ammophila*. *M. sinensis* 'Graziella', 'Morning Light' or 'Flamingo' are particularly suitable for large pots as they are lower growing than some

Frost damage is always more noticeable in exposed sites.

cultivars, thus not so easily blown over. For very exposed roof gardens, provided that you can secure some type of anchor (such as a steel bar) to a wall or the roof itself, lashing pots to it with lorry-ties may be the only solution.

Plants Tolerant of Exposure

Trees and Shrubs

Arctostaphylos uva-ursi
Berberis darwinii
Cytissus
Elaeagnus
Erica (all)
Hamamelis virginiana
Hippophae rhamnoides
Juniperus procumbens
Lavatera
Mahonia (many)
Philadelphus
Spirea
Tamarisk
Taxus baccata
Ulex

Herbaceous Plants

Armeria
Aubretia
Bergenia
Cheiranthus cheri
Dwarf Iris
Erysimum
Lathyrus latifolius
Limonum latifolium
Linum perenne
Matthiola
Meconopsis cambrica
Papaver
Rhodiola rosea
Sedum (all)

Grasses

Ammophila arenaria
Briza media
Calamagrostis x 'Karl Foerster'
Miscanthus sinensis
Stipa tenacissima

Fruit

Damson
Myrobalan or cherry plum

Vegetables

Broad beans, particularly dwarf cultivar 'The Sutton'
Cabbage
Carrots
Garlic
Kale
Leeks
Parsley
Parsnips
Salads (tougher or lower growing, e.g. Claytonia, cos lettuce, lamb's lettuce and oriental brassicas)
Salsify, scorzonera
Sprouting broccoli
Turnips

POLLUTION AND CONTAMINATION

Inner city gardens can suffer from the effects of pollutants, mostly those caused by vehicle exhausts, particularly diesel particulates and hydrogen sulphide generated by catalytic converters running at less than peak efficiency. Likewise rural areas downwind from large conurbations can also suffer, when sulphur dioxide particles transform to complex summer smogs which often fall as a toxic dew in still, warm weather.

Pollution damage is most visible on soft new foliage. The dark brown or black discolorations can superficially resemble a fungal attack, but the location of damage, closest to roadsides or prevailing winds, and with a mixture of species attacked simultaneously make diagnosis easier.

Some plants, in particular the Japanese maples, and most *Abies* species will not tolerate polluted air. Choose hardy species with thick leaves to withstand temporary insults, or some of the tough Victorian favourites which became popular because of their enduring qualities, such as hollies, the ever-present cherry laurel or peonies, which were resistant to soot and coal-fired smogs. For modern roadside conditions, *Ginkgo biloba* is one of the most tolerant.

Other plants with good pollution tolerance include the evergreen *Elaeagnus pungens*, with delicate silver-embossed white blooms in late autumn which scent the air for yards around it, or its variegated form, 'Maculata', or its close cousin *E. umbellata*, the silverberry, with leaves which look to be formed from hammered tinfoil when young, strangely beautiful twigs with copper and bronze raised dots and small brilliant red berries set with silver speckles. *Elaeagnus pungens* makes a good hedge, or large shrub, but *E. umbellata* is best grown as a small, umbrella-shaped tree, pruned carefully to reveal one or more twisting, divided trunks with a tracery of thin branches, sheltering more delicate plants such as hellebores and anemones underneath.

A more worrying problem for vegetable or fruit growers is contaminated soil, usually from former industrial sites or orchards. (Paris Green, an arsenic compound, was used extensively in the

The insignificant flowers of Elaeagnus pungens *will perfume the air for several feet around the bush in early September and continue intermittently until Christmas, if there are few frosts.*

early part of the twentieth century: in some places surprisingly high levels of soil arsenic resulted from this practice.) If you suspect there may be a problem with your soil because of the site's history, you might wish to have a professional soil analysis for toxic metal residues or pesticide levels taken if you intend to be largely self-sufficient. Bear in mind that natural levels of minerals in soil can be surprisingly high, and that levels toxic to humans are often toxic to plants as well, so with a healthy weed population your soil is probably safe.

PH levels influence the uptake of pollutants, particularly the heavy metals, by growing plants. Lead, for example, is almost totally immobile in the soil, and only adsorbed by plant roots in very acidic conditions, pH4 and below, where growth of all but a few specialist species is normally suppressed. Copper, cadmium, mercury and to a lesser extent nickel and fluorine behave similarly.

Generally, the health benefits of eating really fresh produce are greater than the very much smaller risk of problems connected with food grown on contaminated soil. What you eat from the garden will usually only be a relatively small part of your total diet over a lifetime, and health scares should not cause you to stop growing vegetables or fruit.

Contamination of fruit or vegetables by disease-causing bacteria is a less well-known but more likely

Annual Echium vulgare *hybrids are a magnet for bees.*

Ragged robin fills in the gaps between the paving slabs around this small pond designed with wildlife in mind.

form of poisoning, with *Salmonella, Escherichia coli, Listeria* and *Cryptosporidium* all being possible causes of food poisoning, having rarely been found in vegetables or fruit. Here, common sense in both kitchen and garden is the best resort. Many of the problems have been linked to a water supply which has become contaminated with human or animal waste, so don't pee in the garden (except on the compost heap where there are sufficient bugs to destroy any parasites you might harbour). Stack manure for at least twelve months before using it, and don't grow salad crops on land which has been recently manured. Pick food as you want it and cook it as soon as possible after picking (it'll taste better that way too.) Don't keep hot and cold food close together. Wash vegetables and fruit well before eating, in addition to washing your hands before a meal.

WET SITES

Soils which retain moisture during hot summers are rightly prized, but those which suffer from permanent waterlogging are less desirable. Anaerobic micro-organisms (which can live without oxygen) are less active in the soil than most of the normal soil microflora, and have less benefit to plants. Clay soils which are wet for months at a time may become 'gleyed', foul smelling, and blue, green or brick red in colour from the development of iron compounds.

Wet sites contribute to much damage from root-rots, frost damage and windthrow.

In very wet places, digging trenches up to 2ft (60cm) deep will enable a wider range of plants to survive. Less extreme soils can be assisted with a handful of coarse gravel around the roots of plants which require better drainage.

Bamboos which are confined to clumps on drier sites often become alarmingly invasive on a damp soil, and are best restricted by planting in some form of large deep container sunk below the soil surface: field drain pipes if sufficiently large in diameter are very good, as are large bore steel pipes. The only sure-fire way I have ever found of keeping an athletic bamboo in place on a damp clay soil was to wrap it round with a double concentric circle of industrial conveyer belt, buried vertically 4ft (1.3m) deep with the bamboo in the middle. *Chusquea culeou, Phyllostachys edulis* and *P. nigra* all have edible young shoots, if you feel inclined to control your more rampant species via the kitchen.

Plants Tolerant of Damp

These plants enjoy a damp but not permanently waterlogged site.

Trees and Shrubs

Amelanchior
Aronia
Azalea
Betula nigra, B. pubescens
Calycanthus florida
Clethra (all)
Cornus alba, C. stolonifera and cultivars
Mespilus germanica
Salix spp
Sambucus (all)
Sorbus aucuparia and cultivars
Vaccinium
Viburnum opulus

Herbaceous Plants

Aconitum napellus
Ajuga reptans
Amsonia tabernaemontana
Angelica archangelica, A. gigas
Aster lanceolatus
Cimcifuga racemosa
Eupatorium (all)
Filipendula vulgaris 'Aurea'
Iris kaempferi, I. siberica
Ligularia
Lobelia cardinalis, L. siphilitica
Lysmachia (most)
Mimulus luteus
Physalis alkekengi
Polygonum bistorta
Primula alpicola, P. beesiana, P. bulleyana, P. florindae, P. japonica, P. sikkimensis
Rogersia
Sidalcea
Thalictrum dipterocarpum

Grasses

Carex (most species and hybrids)
Deschampsia cespitosa
Eriophorum latifolium
Imperata cylindrica
Melica uniflora
Molina caerulea

Fruit

Blackcurrants
Cranberries (for really waterlogged ground, with acidic soil)
Gooseberry
Morello cherry
Raspberry
Rhubarb
True quince (*Cydonia*)

Vegetables/Herbs

Celery (loves wet feet!)
Chervil
Chives
Horseradish
Lovage (*Levisticum officinale*)
Mints
Parsley
Winter savory

CHAPTER 8

Ecological weed, pest and disease control

WEED CONTROL

Weeds can be divided into various groups – perennial, annual and ephemeral, or alternatively noxious, annoying, tolerated and encouraged.

Ephemeral weeds are annuals with a very short lifecycle, which can be shortened even more by the gardener – in tests, groundsel could have a period of as little as eight weeks from seed to seeding if stimulated sufficiently by regular hoeing. Other ephemeral weeds include annual meadow grass, sun spurge and some willowherbs.

Noxious weeds are always perennial, usually with very deep roots and spread rapidly or produce vast amounts of seed. In the UK ragwort, creeping thistle, giant hogweed and Japanese knotweed are classified in law as noxious weeds, and the land-owner on whose ground these plants grow is legally responsible for both destroying them and ensuring they don't spread.

Annoying weeds have deep but removable roots, spread slightly less rapidly by seed or have a very rapid life cycle. Tolerated weeds include short-lived and shallow-rooted annual subjects such as chickweed, which are easily removed, as well as those perennials which don't spread rapidly. Encouraged weeds are plants attractive to garden-ers, wildife or both, easily pulled out and have just come up in the wrong place.

It has been estimated that in every cubic inch of topsoil from anywhere in the UK there are an average of at least twelve weed seeds (a large pro-portion of these being fat hen, *Chenopodium album*, which was cultivated, being edible, in the Iron Age) so the chances of a totally weed-free garden are slim.

Hoeing is probably the most efficient method of weed removal but must be done regularly, at least once a week. If the weather is at all damp the weed seedlings should be removed to prevent them from re-rooting: those not in flower can be composted. Hoeing will gradually weaken persistent weeds such as lesser bindweed, but all root fragments should be removed promptly. For open soil, a Dutch or reciprocating hoe is fine, but for close working between plants a draw hoe gives better control. As a patch of soil is agitated by hoeing, fresh weed seeds will be drawn up to the surface for some time – the old saying 'one year's seeding, seven year's weeding' is only too true.

Hand weeding can be more effective on small patches, among seedlings or ground cover plants, though it is time consuming. Removal of seedling roots is usually better than with hoeing, and natu-rally very good control can be exercised.

Digging out of noxious and annoying weeds can be effective, particularly those such as brambles, docks, creeping buttercups or nettles, provided the entire root can be removed. For difficult or persistent weeds such as creeping thistle or lesser bindweed, digging can make things worse by creat-ing several fresh points of regeneration apart from the original weed.

You can compost perennial weed roots and flowering annuals in a hot heap (as mentioned in Chapter 4). Alternative noxious weed disposal methods include putting them in a securely sealed compost bin or dustbin with the lid on for a minimum of eighteen months, or composting after soaking the weeds thoroughly for a few weeks in a bucket or tank of water.

Really deep-rooted weeds should be regarded as a valuable source of trace elements rather than as a problem: they bring up vital nutrients from deep

One of the gardener's best friends, a ladybird larva.

layers of soil and, once decomposed, these can be applied to the soil safely.

Around the Edges

Weeds which creep in from next door are the bane of keen gardener's life, and have the most dedicated organic growers contemplating herbicides in despair. If you are determined to use no weedkiller but want to stop bindweed, ground elder and couch grass, burying a 3ft (1m) depth of plastic or butyl rubber sheet vertically in the ground will prevent these escaping for several years. Be warned – it won't stop bamboo or Japanese knotweed, which will require copper-impregnated membrane, several inches of solid rock or sheets of corrugated iron!

Flame Guns

For rapid control of weeds in cracks in paving, long-rooted perennials along wall edges or on aggregate, flame guns (powered by propane or paraffin) or the smaller spot weeders (which usually run on small propane cylinders) are invaluable. They have no toxic residues, are useful for controlling seed spread and quickly sterilize tools which have been used to dig up diseased plants. One of the ultimate big boy's toys, they give a great feeling of power to the user and can be very effective in skilled hands. Regular use of a flame gun on hard surfaces will kill off weed seeds and so lessen the need to use it.

When using a flame gun, choose a bright, windy day. The object is not to blast the offending weed into a pile of cinders but to stress it as much as possible by a single pass of flame. This will damage the leaf surfaces so that it rapidly desiccates through the cut edges. Five or six days later, repeat the process, by which time the weed will be severely weakened if not permanently destroyed. Some long-rooted weeds like creeping thistle might need flaming regularly for a season before they give up.

The global disadvantages of using fossil fuels for a job which can be done by hand are obvious, but for large areas flame guns may be the only practical method. Long term, the ideal would be to reduce the amount of hard surface with cracks in it which need weeding, or sow them with a more desirable plant which would suppress the weeds without being over-invasive, such as *Pratia peduncularis*, which withstands occasional treading.

Mulches

Mulching can either reduce or increase weeds, depending on the nature of the mulch and the soil. While spreading a fertile substance such as garden compost or leafmould onto a plot with perennial weeds lurking below the surface will encourage them to grow with renewed energy, covering them with a light-suppressing layer will cause them to weaken and die.

Don't use carpet for ground clearance, as their often toxic dyes pollute and persist in soil, and even undyed carpet is almost impossible to dig through once overgrown, because the fibres don't always decompose. Carpet squares are very useful as temporary protection, such as under fruiting strawberries to keep berries clean, for making kneeling mats, or covering compost heaps to retain warmth.

Hay should also be avoided as a mulch material, because it always contains weed seeds, and can cause nitrogen deficiency as it decomposes. Semi-decomposed or 'mow-burnt' hay, which is often offered to gardeners cheaply, being unfit for animal feed, contains fewer weed seeds but is still better used on the compost heap than on borders.

Long-term use of cardboard, especially when combined with crushed sea-shells as a mulch, has been shown to increase the number of beneficial fungi, particularly those which attack plant pathogens. For best results, the cardboard needs to be in place for at least six months, preferably more, when the soil is warm and damp.

Recommended Sustainable Mulching Materials

Material	Where to Use	Advantages	Disadvantages
Bark chips	Under shrubs, trees and around perennials	Weed suppressant Long life (2–3 years) Helps improve soil as it breaks down Easy to handle May help frost protection	Expensive Possible N deficiency when decomposing Sometimes contains splinters
Cardboard	General weed control Ground clearing	Usually free Easy to spread Light to handle Stops most perennial weeds if left on for 12 months plus	Needs weighing down or blows away Lifespan (18 months or less) Doesn't improve soil structure, no nutrients May encourage slugs
Garden compost	Vegetable plot (in rotation) Around fruit bushes, trees, shrubs	Free garden waste-disposal and recycling Improves soil structure May help frost protection Increases beneficial life in soil Slow release nutrients	May contain weeds, disease or pests if badly made Can encourage moles (feeding on extra worms) Heavy Doesn't stop weeds
Lawn mowings	In thin layers around shrubs, soft fruit, rows of vegetables	Free, easily available Improves soil structure Slow release nitrogen in small amounts Deters carrot and cabbage root fly Prevents carrot green-top	If put on too thickly turns slimy and heats up, scorching plant roots Possible N deficiency when decomposes In wet weather encourages disease and slugs
Newspaper	General weed clearing Summer soft fruit mulch, topped with other material, e.g. straw, lawn mowings	Free, easily available Easy to lay Light to handle Retains soil moisture Biodegradable	Must be weighted down with lawn mowings or straw – can still blow away in strong winds May encourage slugs
Plastic semi-permeable membrane	General ground clearing Permanent plantings (if covered with other material) Lining for coldframes or pathways in polytunnels	Long lasting Good weed control Easy to lay Lightweight Retains soil moisture	Expensive Some weeds can penetrate, especially twitch and bindweed Difficult to remove once laid, mulched & planted through Needs regular sweeping to remove weed seeds and soil if uncovered
Straw	Over newspaper as general weed clearing As temporary mulch under soft fruits Overnight frost protection for potatoes etc. in late spring	Lightweight Cheap Easy to lay Biodegradable	Poor weed control on its own – may contain weed seeds Possibility of contamination with weedkiller residues Can encourage slugs Blows away in dry windy weather

PESTS AND DISEASES

There are always going to be problems in every-body's garden from time to time. Some you can influence, in the same way as exercise, eating healthily and getting enough sleep will help your own body stay fit, but some are inevitable, like catching the common cold. Many are linked with certain cultural or weather conditions, for example during wet summers there are likely to be more attacks of potato blight and increased mollusc infestation than in a dry season. Like crowded soldiers suffering outbreaks of typhoid fever in the trenches, badly grown plants – overcrowded, stressed, over or underfed or just badly drained – are just waiting for disease to strike.

ABOVE: *Frogs are excellent controllers of slugs and small snails.*

BELOW: *Caterpillar of the large white butterfly or cabbage white.*

Keep your plants healthy by avoiding excessive use of fertilizers and manures, which lead to 'soft' sappy, vigorous growth, delectably attractive to feeding insects and easily infected by disease. Garden compost, leafmould and the occasional application of extra potash from comfrey leaves or municipal compost are all most soils will need, unless you practise very intensive vegetable cultivation. Yes, you will have smaller, less prolific plants, but they will be grown 'hard' with larger root systems, and firmer cell walls, making them less attractive targets and better able to fight off attack.

Don't try to force plants into growth too soon, or coddle them too much from icy winds and frosts by using fleece. A little cold is a good thing, making sure full dormancy is achieved, although when cold weather is forecast moving pots exposed to high winds to somewhere more sheltered, such as under a hedge or in the lee of a wall, is always a good plan.

Wide spacings between plants ensure good air circulation, and help ward off fungal problems. Improving drainage by adding grit and leafmould to heavy soils, growing in raised beds and removing saucers from under pots in wet weather or during winter can all help reduce disease.

Confuse pests and attract predators by mixing flowers in with your vegetables – this not only gives some beautiful effects, but blurs the perception of flying pests, who instinctively look for the shadow of a plant against bare soil, or home in on others by scent and taste. Open flowers bring in hoverflies, lacewings and other insect-eaters, while a melange of leaf textures, colours and smells makes for a glorious muddle. This is the true origin of companion planting, rather than any mysterious blending of root exudates or essential oils to deter bugs.

Lastly, don't expect all your plants to look perfect throughout their lives. Minor spots or holes on leaves can be regarded as unsightly but not life-threatening, in the same way as teenage acne, and just as many humans develop mild arthritis or rheumatism as they age, mature trees often suffer a few permanent imperfections as they get older without serious effect on their general health.

Pests

Pests can be controlled by barriers, traps, deterrents or biological control, as well as by poisoning.

Aphids (Greenfly)

Aphids come in all shapes, sizes and colours, not all green: they are often very specific to particular plants, but some, like the peach-potato aphid, are omnivorous. Young, soft, succulent spring growth is especially attractive. As they plug into a plant's sapstream, they excrete a sweet substance (honeydew) continuously, which encourages the growth of sooty moulds on leaves below, turning leaves black and sticky.

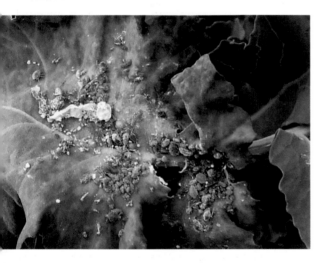

Cabbage aphids. In the lower corner of the picture, golden globules of parasitized aphids mark the presence of a natural predator, Aphidus, *a parasitic wasp.*

Aphids carry a range of other plant diseases, especially viruses, from one plant to another. They are often protected by ants who farm them for their honeydew, and guard them from predators such as ladybirds.

Aphids are an important food source for all sorts of other creatures, from birds through hoverflies, wasps, ladybirds and lacewings, and will normally be controlled in a short time as predators home in on this new food supply. They multiply so fast that a large population forms before the predators can catch up, so speed is essential when dealing with these pests.

A small outbreak can be easily squashed or washed off with a water jet, but larger infestations should be treated with a spray of insecticidal soap or micronized rape oil, depending on what plant's being attacked. (Rape oil is unsuitable for some plants, especially those with hairy leaves.)

Biological controls such as ladybirds, parasitic wasps and lacewings are sold to control aphids, if you don't have a large enough natural supply – these are very effective. A ladybird larva will eat 250–400 aphids, depending on size and species, while a lacewing can devour even more before turning into an adult.

Some success has been observed with spraying plants with strong smelling substances, such as garlic tea, neem extract and chick-pea exudates: these are not all legal as insecticides in all countries, although they appear to deter aphids from feeding. They may kill predators as well as the pest.

Winged aphids can be prevented from attacking seedling plants by a fine mesh cover.

Cabbage Root Fly

The cabbage root fly can be a serious pest in some districts, yet rarely make an appearance in others. It attacks all members of the brassica family, from stocks and wallflowers to cabbage, kale and broccoli.

The adult fly resembles a small horsefly and produces up to three generations of small, maggot-like larvae which devour the stem and roots, causing stunted growth, wilting in dry weather or total collapse of otherwise healthy looking plants. Seedlings and transplants are equally affected.

Prevention is simple, by use of a fine mesh cover for seed-rows, or root-mats (traditionally home-made from old carpet underlay, cardboard or rubber car-mats) which are at least 4in (10cm) square, fitting tightly around the plant's roots and extending a few inches beyond the stem. Mulching around the base of young brassicas with a thin layer of grass-clippings, renewed every time you mow the lawn, will also work well, making it too much of an effort for the fly to dig through to lay eggs.

Dig over ground where an attack has occurred, to expose larvae to predatory birds.

Intercropping with dwarf French beans or low growing legumes such as fenugreek is claimed to be useful as it disguises the outline of a brassica seedling from the air.

Carrot Root Fly

Protecting carrots with fine mesh netting.

Carrot root fly rarely shows except when the first roots are harvested. True, a slight reddening of the leaves or a minor lack of vigour may appear along a row, but nothing that a possible unevenness of fertility or water stress in dry weather might not explain, until pulling the plants up reveals a crazy tattoo patterning of dark brown tunnels throughout the root, many with tiny cream maggots in residence. Parsley and parsnips also suffer.

The female carrot fly detects its target by scent, so can be confused if you intercrop carrots with strong smelling plants such as onions – but these need to be actively growing to release their volatile compounds. Tests show that four rows of onions are required to protect a single row of carrots. Other smelly plant possibilities include fenugreek and basil.

To avoid attracting carrot fly, sow thinly to avoid the need for thinning; weed carrots only in dull windy or wet weather, when the insects don't fly; and bury any carrot tops deep in the compost heap.

The best control is by barrier – covering the crop with a fine mesh net as soon as leaves emerge, laid over the seedbed and spaded in to lie loosely over the row, or secured over a mini-tunnel. It must be left in place for the life of the crop to be effective.

Certain cultivars, principally 'Sytan' and 'Flyaway' are promoted for being resistant to fly attack. Some gardeners claim this is due to their flavour.

Caterpillars and Cutworms

Cutworms are soil-living moth larvae, which do considerable damage to young seedlings by biting stems off at ground level without damaging the leaves. They are often nocturnal in their feeding habits and can remain unseen, feeding for months below soil level.

The first sign of cutworm is usually when you find a row of newly transplanted seedlings lying flat on the ground from overnight attack, or discover the larvae – which may be any colour from grubby off-white through patterned browns and greys to brilliant green – as you turn the soil. In late winter to spring the larvae turn to torpedo-shaped pupae, which are usually shiny brown or orange in colour.

Caterpillars which feed above ground come in all sorts of shapes and sizes, but only a few do serious damage to plants and can often be regarded as a nuisance rather than a serious pest. The exceptions most commonly encountered by gardeners are those which attack all the brassicas, from cabbages to nasturtiums – large and small white butterflies,

Cutworm caterpillar making a journey above ground as it seeks a suitable place to pupate.

cabbage moths whose larvae are dull green and lurk on the inner white midrib of the leaves, plus the dull brownish diamondback moth caterpillars, fortunately rare except in the South. There's also the infuriating group of tortrix moths, whose very small greenish caterpillars link leaves together with silk before devouring them, particularly a nuisance on houseplants.

Cutworms in open ground are best controlled by regular soil cultivation and subsequent exposure of larvae. They make excellent additions to the bird table, or can simply be gathered up and squashed. Examining container plants with a torch after dark often reveals cutworms coming up to feed, when they can be picked off and killed.

Hand-picking of individual surface-living caterpillars is fine for small infestations (avoid handling very hairy caterpillars which can cause skin irritation), but impractical on very large outbreaks.

Netting over brassicas will prevent butterflies from laying their neat patches of tiny golden eggs, but they are very determined in their efforts to reach the leaves, even to the extent of squeezing their abdomens through fine mesh to push the eggs into place – so make sure there are no gaps they can creep through with folded wings.

Biological control is ecologically sound and effective, but the larvae must be in contact with the active ingredient for best results, and they do not die immediately, although they stop feeding within a few days after application. Seeing live pests wriggling after spraying may make some gardeners feel that the control isn't working – be patient!

Bacillus thuringensis is naturally occurring fungus which kills the caterpillars that feed or walk over sprayed leaves. Heavy rain can wash it off leaves, so it would need to be reapplied frequently in wet weather. An alternative is a nematode (microscopic eelworm) spray, which can be applied in damp cloudy weather, which kills the larvae by feeding inside them.

Natural controls include solitary wasps which parasitize large white larvae, as well as birds and predatory ground beetles. Common wasps eat a great number of caterpillars, mostly early in the year when they are feeding their own young, and for this reason queen wasps should be left undisturbed when they emerge in spring.

Codling moth pheromone trap.

Codling Moth

When your apples have holes in their sides which reach through the flesh to the core, codling moth larvae have hatched, fed and gone. Pears are also attacked sometimes.

The female moths are wingless and cannot fly, so crawl up the trunks of fruit trees in late autumn to lay their eggs, like a small lace bracelet on young branches, which hatch as fruits form. These eat the fruit from the inside, mostly around the core, then burrow outwards and fall to the ground and pupate.

The male moths hatch before the females, and will fertilize them as they emerge, seeking each one by scent. Because of this they can be trapped by an artificial female moth pheromone on a sticky trap, which should be placed in the tree during the flying season, from mid May till early September. One trap will protect several trees. The lure will need renewing every six weeks or so, and should be removed once moths no longer come to it, to avoid trapping anything else which might be attracted to the dead moths.

Flea Beetle

These small beetles can be very worrying for the vegetable grower, causing young seedlings to appear almost transparent with perforations on the leaves where the insects feed. They attack brassicas mostly but not exclusively and can be seen either by the damaged leaves or as a horde of tiny bugs leaping away from disturbed plants. They are worst in hot dry weather. In the UK they are common in early to mid summer, as the oil-seed rape crops on which they feed have gone to seed or been harvested.

Once most seedlings are more than a few inches/centimetres high they are no longer susceptible, so the first method of defence is to encourage seedlings to grow rapidly by improved growing conditions – providing fertile, non-capped soil, increased warmth by using fleece in cold spells, and watering well if dry.

Holding a yellow sticky trap directly over the plants while rattling the leaves with a stick will trap a sizeable number of pests, and covering rows of seed as it's sown with fine mesh cloches will prevent attack.

Larger Pests – Deer, Squirrels, Rabbits and Birds

Town gardeners have just as much cause to curse the cat which carefully rakes up lettuce seedlings to defecate on them, or the holes left by urban foxes digging up where bonemeal has been spread as do country folk waking up to find an absence of roses or carrots caused by nocturnal visits from deer or rabbits. Some precautions work – the best way of deterring other cats is to keep a dog or tomcat of your own – and some don't, such as putting

Rabbit damage to carrots.

mothballs or empty milk bottles in runs to deter moles.

Scented deterrents include a variety of vile stinking substances, from Jeyes fluid to lion dung, which often repel humans as effectively as other animals. Another is scattering sweepings of human hair in areas where deer or rabbits are likely to enter the garden. As this should be taken from people who don't live in the immediate neighbourhood, nor artificially coloured, a barber's in the next town would be a suitable source.

Other deterrents are easier on the nostrils, such as hanging up unwanted CDs, windmills and plastic strips to blow or crackle in the wind. All deterrents rely on novelty value, and will need to be moved around the ground or just changed regularly. For the determined pest, if money is no object, you can purchase a remote controlled sensor, attached to the mains, which squirts water at an approaching foe.

The best but most expensive defence is a barrier, at least until plants are large enough to be unaffected. Rabbits can be stopped by a 3ft (1m) height of wire mesh, with an additional 12in (30cm) mesh buried at a 45° angle outwards or on a larger scale by electric fencing run from a car battery, while deer will need a permanent fence of at least 6ft (2m) to deny them entry.

Squirrels and other rodents, being able to climb, are more difficult to deter, and here the barriers have to be local, such as burying wire mesh over bulbs or pots of seeds to prevent them from being eaten, or scattering prickly prunings of gorse or berberis among tender seedlings, which also works well for cats. Wrapping a cage of wire netting around particularly attractive plants may be the only method of protection for the persistent nibbler. Rodent teeth can deal with surprisingly thick wire and you may have to resort to weldmesh for protecting special favourites.

Young trees and fruit bushes should be protected using heavy-duty plastic tree-guards, but check them occasionally for tightness around growing stems, and for vole damage: voles can squeeze beneath the plastic to munch on the bark in safety.

Netting brassicas to protect them from pigeons is a necessity in most rural districts and in quite a

Netting brassicas against pigeons.

few urban ones as well. London suffers from the added problem of the introduced rose-ringed parakeet which flocks in large numbers – these can strip a tree bare in an hour. Temporary supports can be erected using sticks or canes with netting draped over to save fruit bushes from attack, but winter vegetables will need a more solidly supported cover, able to stand up to winter winds or avoid being crushed below snow. Fruit cages are expensive and often lead to bushes being grown in closer contact than is ideal, so if you decide to invest in one, make sure it's the biggest you can afford.

Trapping is usually efficient, but has to be done well. Before you start trapping, realize that if your garden is a desirable habitat you will find that as soon as one occupant of the territory has been removed, another will replace it. For example, in a single small garden as many as thirty grey squirrels may be removed in one season before you notice any lessening of damage.

If you catch it, whatever it is, if it's a pest, it must be killed quickly and cleanly. Find somebody who can show you how to set a mouse or mole trap if you don't know how yourself. Breakback traps are fast and efficient if set properly. Live traps for small animals such as mice are inhumane, because the creatures die of stress and hunger or thirst overnight. Do not be tempted to release live-trapped animals away from home. This is both

cruel, as they will be defenceless when attacked by other members of their species because they are away from their territory, and in the case of grey squirrels, illegal in the UK.

Sawfly

The sawflies are a group of usually small two-winged flies which are insignificant as adults but have destructive larvae. Each species of sawfly is host-specific, but can be very damaging on the plants which are attacked.

The larvae are caterpillar-like, with dark heads and pale green or grey bodies: they feed on leaf edges or undersides, making them difficult to see until damage is advanced, and arrive in swarms which can strip a bush within days. Commonly encountered are gooseberry sawfly (which also attacks red and white currants), rose sawfly and Solomon's seal sawfly. Handpicking of pest or individual leaves, depending on larval size works on a few small plants, or use insecticidal soap for heavy infestations. Garlic infusions work well as a preventative and deterrent. Gooseberry sawfly can have up to six generations a year, but most of the other species have only one or two. As the pests overwinter in the soil below the infected plants, regular hoeing of the soil during the winter is helpful, to expose pupae to birds and frosts.

Rose sawfly larvae.

SLUGS AND SNAILS

During winter or long drought spells during summer look out for snails hiding in cracks and crevices, where they can be easily destroyed.

There must be as many ways of slug control as there are gardeners. Here are just a few of the more effective...

During the winter, check all cracks and crevices in paving, and tidy garden debris where snails gather in groups to hibernate. They can be squashed and put on the bird table, where they will be eagerly devoured.

In spring and summer, go into the garden on mild damp evenings with a torch and destroy as many slugs or snails as you can find. Remember, one less snail in spring means around 300 fewer in the autumn.

Spread rough or fine textured material such as powdered eggshell or various commercial compounds around plants, which the slugs are supposed to dislike crossing.

Surround seedlings with bottle-cloches. This creates a physical barrier – make sure there are no slugs inside before fitting it.

Lay thin copper mesh or strips around pots or groups of seedlings, which gives the creatures an electric shock when they cross it. This is most effective when wrapped around pots, particularly of such slug-magnets as hostas, but possibly less so on open ground, where they can burrow beneath the copper.

Encircle plants with bran. This works well in dry weather – the slugs are supposed to gorge on it until they burst – but it's less effective in wet conditions.

Heavy use of bran can give rise to problems of temporary nitrogen deficiency, in the same way as digging in a green manure, while the soil micro-organisms break it down.

Sink dishes filled with slops begged from your local pub. This kills by drowning their intoxicated visitors. Keep them raised slightly above ground to avoid killing ground beetles as well as slugs.

Encourage slugs to come to bait such as downturned grapefruit halves. They need regular nightly checking, with the removal and disposal of their contents. However much you may dislike your neighbours, don't dispose of your snails by throwing them over the fence: they have a homing instinct, and will return, hungrier than before, from considerable distances. Squash them or feed them to ducks in a local park.

Encourage predators, such as ground beetles, by leaving slates or tiles scattered across bare soil to act as beetle refuges during the day.

Dig a pond, or build a hibernaculum to encourage frogs, toads and newts which eat slugs and their eggs.

Leave a small gap at the base of all fences, so hedgehogs can travel from one garden to another, munching as they go. Provide hedgehogs with a safe place to hibernate, as well as putting out food and water for them during summer. Hedgehogs can't digest bread and milk, so give them a special dry mix or just plain catfood.

Use aluminium-based slug pellets, harmless to other wildlife, rather than those based on toxic metaldehyde.

In spring, apply biological control – nematodes – on areas planted with susceptible crops. These will work for about six weeks giving time for the plants to become big enough to cope with damage.

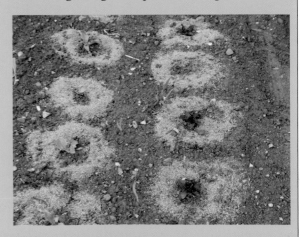

Scattering a ring of bran around young plants works well against slugs or snails, especially in dry weather.

Vine Weevil

Vine weevil larvae are serious garden pests, causing devastating destruction to plants with a central crown such as *Primula, Bergenia, Heuchera, Cyclamen* or strawberries. Individual larvae are creamish, sluggish moving and caterpillar-like with a dark head, forming a C-shaped curl: they grow up to ½in (2cm) long. The adults cause small notches in evergreen leaves, feeding overnight on evergreens such as camellias, ivy or *Viburnum tinus*. The black, dusty-looking adults, all parthenogenetic females, have shallow parallel grooves down their backs, and move slowly: if disturbed they play dead, lying on their backs with legs folded.

Adults are active in spring and late summer, larvae or pupae being found all year round. On warm summer nights they can often be found crawling along paths or on walls, by careful search with a torch, when they can be picked off and killed.

Larvae can be countered with a drench of predatory nematodes, provided soil temperatures are above 45°F (7°C): this is effective prevention for containers but expensive in large areas of open ground, when cultural control such as encouraging ground beetles or regular soil exposure work best.

In greenhouses, sticky bands around the legs of greenhouse staging can prevent weevils climbing up to attack pots on a bench above.

Whitefly

Whitefly in the garden can be a number of species but the most infuriating is probably the cabbage whitefly, which forms dense colonies on the inner leaves of brassicas, particularly in cool weather. There are natural predators, such as the parasitic wasp *Aphidus*, which attack the creatures in warmer parts of the year but in winter the most effective control for major attacks is by spraying weekly with insecticidal soap.

Lower leaves with whitefly can be picked off and buried deep in the compost heap, or in dry weather a quick blast of water with a hosepipe is an effective method of removing small patches of cabbage whitefly.

Remove old brassica crops before planting out

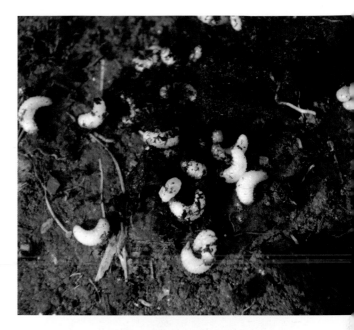

Vine weevil larvae. (Photo: Rhoda Nottridge)

young seedlings, and don't grow old and new brassicas side by side, even in a rotation.

Whitefly under cover are usually the glasshouse whitefly, which feeds on the underside of leaves, sucking sap in huge colonies, leading to a mottled appearance of the upperside, and leaves withering. Severe infestations can be fatal. All types of plant are attacked, particular favourites being tomatoes, cucumbers and many houseplants.

Good hygiene is the key, by cleaning down greenhouses thoroughly with plenty of soap and water in spring before starting growing again, or if plants such as vines are present, fumigation with a sulphur candle during the winter when all are dormant.

Hanging yellow sticky traps above plants will catch small numbers of whitefly, but when numbers increase dramatically, it's time to use biological control or insecticidal soap. Remove the traps before introducing predators, or you'll catch them too. Bio-controls include a parasitic wasp, *Encarsia*, which needs minimum air temperatures of 50°F (10°C) before it is active, or a beetle, *Delphastus*, which works when conditions are hotter – up to 70–82°F (21–28°C). Both of these can both be bought mail-order.

Woolly Aphid

If you find a waxy tufted white deposit during the growing season on the stems and trunks of apple (including crab-apples), hawthorn, *Pyracantha*, *Cotoneaster* and relatives, which if rubbed with a finger turns reddish as the brown aphids generating the fluff are killed, you've got woolly aphids. Galls may form and splits in the bark develop, causing dieback or distorted leaves. The pest overwinters in cracks in the bark or in galls. Some cultivars such as 'Cornish Aromatic' seem more susceptible than others.

Woolly aphid attacks most woody members of the Rosaceae *family.*

Small patches can be scrubbed off using a toothbrush, or cut off and burned. For large infestations, consider using a winter wash of plant based oils. There is a natural predator, a parasitic wasp, but it is rarely present in sufficient numbers to kill all the aphids.

Diseases

Diseases can be controlled to some extent by cultural controls, by selectively breeding for resistance (although this is liable to change over time), or by chemical methods.

Try to practise some measure of quarantine – if you have an allotment, keep a separate set of allotment-only tools and boots, or use a disinfectant dip before using them on the home garden. In working your way round the garden, deal with diseased plants last, to avoid spreading contamination on your hands or clothing. Sterilize secateurs or knives by wiping the blades with surgical spirit after pruning an infected plant, and wash your hands well with soap and water before touching a healthy one.

Apple Scab and Canker

Scab and canker attack apples (including ornamental *Malus spp*) and pears. Most old apple trees will have some infection, but often crop well despite it.

In scab, the leaves develop dark brown blotches and may fall early. Infected fruits have dark patches which may become corky and split but don't decay. Stems may blister and develop brownish-green pustules in early spring.

Canker shows as dark distorted depressions on twigs or cracked shrunken lesions on stems, which kill the branches above if they ring the limb. Fruit cracks, but doesn't discolour, and some may dry out, remaining mummified on the tree after the leaves have fallen.

Both diseases are worst in wet cold springs and develop quickly in cold damp summers. They spread in wind and rain from overwintering spores, either from mummified fruit, fallen leaves or lesions in the bark. Canker can be spread from hawthorn

Apple scab on foliage.

or poplar windbreaks, or nearby hedges, as well as neighbouring fruit trees.

Resistant cultivars include 'Annie Elizabeth', 'Arthur Turner', 'Falstaff', 'Katy', 'Lord Lambourne', 'Newton Wonder' and 'Sunset'.

Don't grow apples in wet heavy soils or in regions of very high rainfall. Growing trees in grass, or applying a straw mulch below the trunks, helps prevent rain splash spreading infection from the ground.

To limit the disease, sweep up all fallen leaves under trees, remove and burn all infected twigs and prune to encourage good air circulation. In less than perfect conditions, grow trees as a fan or espalier to maximize air flow. Remove mummified fruits promptly and destroy them.

Older trees, if cropping well and otherwise healthy, should be treated minimally, but avoid planting young trees nearby.

Blight

Blight affects tomatoes and potatoes, attacking crops in warm wet weather and spreading very rapidly.

Potato blight.

The disease first appears as black or brown markings on leaves and stems, with white fungal threads visible on the leaf underside, especially in damp weather. The whole plant can collapse and die back within days. Tomato fruits show

Potato blight on tomato fruits.

brownish discolouration or may become leathery and shrivel later on, especially in storage. Tubers become sunken, firm and discoloured throughout, even after appearing perfect when harvested: they frequently develop secondary rots, turning to smelly, slimy mush. The disease overwinters on infected plant tissue, surviving either as seeds from infected tomatoes which germinate in greenhouses, polytunnels or compost heaps, or as buried potatoes which sprout early in the year.

Select blight-resistant potato cultivars – the 'Sarpo' cultivars, from crosses with *Solanum phujarea*, are most blight resistant – and only use certified seed potatoes from a reputable source. There are as yet no blight-resistant tomato cultivars.

Destroy any self-set tomatoes or potatoes, and earth up potato crops well to protect tubers as they form. If blight appears on leaves, remove them and compost quickly: in severe attacks, cut stems to ground level and wait three weeks for the spores on the soil to die before harvesting.

Alternatively, spray with Bordeaux mixture at weekly intervals from the first sign of infection for three weeks.

If you have tubers from blighted plants don't store them close to those from unaffected ones, and use them first. Green tomatoes which have no dark markings cropped from infected plants can be used safely for chutney. Don't save seed from blighted tomatoes.

Blackleg

Blackleg is a seed-carried and soil-borne disease of potatoes, and is worst in wet seasons when plants become waterlogged. Even with the best quality seed potatoes, a small number of tubers will be infected. The disease is long-lived in the soil, and can persist in isolated pockets for many years.

The infected plants, which are usually solitary in an otherwise perfect crop, develop a characteristic wilt, with stems bending double: closer inspection shows a blackish to dark brown discolouration of the stem, and tubers may develop a greyish slime.

Don't plant potatoes in very wet sites, and select tolerant cultivars such as 'Orla', 'Kestrel', 'Wilja' or 'Cara'.

Remove and destroy infected plants. Wash tools and boots before working again in a potato crop. Lift healthy potatoes in dry weather to reduce cross infection, and keep them above 39°F (4°C) to prevent further development of disease in store.

Clubroot

Clubroot affects brassicas, particularly cabbages, kale, swedes, candytuft and calabrese.

Seedlings can be attacked and show no symptoms until half-grown. In a row of plants infected by clubroot they appear stunted and blueish or red-tinted: when one is pulled up, the roots are a cancerous mass of swollen distorted tissue. They fail to thrive and produce little or nothing.

It is worst in stressed plants, grown in wet, acidic conditions when there are low levels of organic matter in the soil. It forms resting spores which persist in the soil for long periods and can be transmitted on infected soil carried by boots, tools and also from droppings of animals fed on infected crops. This ailment is caused by a small unicellular organism which is not a true fungus, unlike many other plant diseases, and can be controlled by anti-biotic effects in compost-living organisms.

Regular liming of areas which are intended for brassica crops on acid soils is an important part of clubroot control, as is using garden compost to improve soil fertility and build up micro-organism populations. Remove and destroy infected plants – do not compost – and practise long rotations.

Raise transplants from seed in modules and grow on in modules using proprietary compost before planting out. Some vegetable cultivars are resistant, so study catalogues before choosing seed.

For small gardens, you can try making a tea from cabbage leaves or saving the water in which cabbage has been cooked, then watering it onto soil where another crop has been sown but where clubroot has occurred previously; this has been shown to diminish attack by inducing spore germination without a food supply for the disease to flourish on.

Onion White Rot

Members of the onion family – ornamental alliums, leeks, shallots, chives and garlic as well as onions – suffer from a confusing group of diseases with similar symptoms, but it is important to distinguish between them because of their difference in severity.

The two most severe problems – white rot and onion downy mildew – overwinter in the soil as resting spores, in autumn-sown or perennial crops.

White Rot

In white rot plants which look healthy suddenly turn yellow from the older leaves first then die. Attacks may be limited to a few plants or the entire row. If a plant is pulled up, the roots have died and are covered in a white furry mould, sometimes with tiny black spore bodies resembling poppy seeds among it. These are very persistent and can survive in the soil for over twenty years without a suitable host.

Remove and destroy any diseased plants as soon as seen. Don't compost debris from the rest of the crop – burn them or put them into the dustbin to be high-temperature composted by the council. Sow autumn onions sets late, to avoid infection, and grow them as far away as possible from summer crops. Practise good hygiene – on allotments, if you know there is white rot on the site don't encourage other gardeners to come onto your plot.

Garlic is worst affected by white rot, while leeks

can tolerate the disease. In both white rot and downy mildew there are pro-biotic benefits from the regular use of garden compost in moderate amounts. Spraying a tea made from onion peelings or boiled garlic on the soil in late August and again in early March can induce resting spores to germinate in the absence of host plants, especially if combined with deep cultivations to expose as many spores as possible.

Powdery mildew on courgette plants.

Powdery and Downy Mildews

Powdery mildew is the name given to a number of related fungi which each attack a specific host, but all have similar symptoms. Mildew on one plant will not necessarily infect another species growing close by, but as all mildews require similar conditions to develop, both plants may be affected at the same time. Mildew spores can overwinter in fallen leaves below perennial plants from apples to Michaelmas daisies.

Powdery mildew occurs as a powdery white coating on leaves and stems, rarely flowers. Dry roots, humid still air and nitrogen rich soil which gives soft growth, all predispose to powdery mildew, as do hot dry days and cold nights.

Downy mildew is similar in appearance, but tends to be worse in wet weather, and is also often host-specific. Onion downy mildew can be imported on healthy looking infected sets, or in seed collected from apparently healthy plants, both home-saved and in packets bought from reputable seed companies.

High humidity, cold soil conditions and heavy rain or frequent overwatering encourage downy mildew. Downy mildew often affects young plants, as yellowish patches on leaf uppers with fungal threads visible below. In downy mildew, infected leaves turn yellow from tips down, with pale leaf spots often developing. In humid conditions, leaf spots become covered in fine fungal fuzz, whiteish at first, then brownish-purple. If flowers are infected, little or no seed is produced.

With both diseases, plants may die back, become stunted or stop growing.

Select mildew resistant cultivars wherever possible. Allow plenty of space between plants, mulch to retain moisture and water well in dry conditions. With woody subjects, such as gooseberries or apples, train as a fan or espalier to allow plenty of air to circulate. Protect newly transplanted seedlings with fleece if cold night temperatures are forecast.

Perennial plants should have any infected leaves or stems removed promptly and composted in a hot heap. Divide clump-forming plants regularly, cut back stems as soon as flowers have finished and don't overfeed.

Mildew resistant Michaelmas daisies include *Aster x frikartii* 'Wunder von Staffa', *Aster novi-belgii* 'Climax', 'Remembrance' and 'Little Boy Blue'.

Rose Black Spot

Black spot is probably the most well-known rose ailment, and one which bothers gardeners most. Its spread can be linked directly to the Clean Air Act, because when coal fires were the norm, high levels of atmospheric sulphur kept the spots at bay, but increasing use of gas or electricity for heating meant that sulphur levels in the air fell and the disease could reappear.

Black spot on rose leaves.

Fortunately there are a number of measures which diminish black spot, principally the choice of cultivar: the climbing 'Leaping Salmon', floribunda 'Ice Cream' and the David Austin English rose 'Shakespeare' are all rarely affected, while species such as *Rosa rugosa* are virtually immune. Planting roses as part of a mixed border reduces the chances of infection and spread: so does limiting their feeding and proper pruning.

Black spot is worst in cold damp seasons, on crowded roses growing as a monoculture, with high levels of soil nitrogen and limited air circulation. The spores overwinter on fallen leaves or on the soil surface, and are spread by rainsplash as the new leaves develop, or in the wind in wet conditions.

Remove infected leaves once seen: new growth will soon make up any deficits. Rake up any fallen leaves and either compost them in a hot heap or destroy them. During the autumn and winter, remove all fallen leaves from below rose bushes and prune carefully to create open, cup-shaped bushes. In spring apply low-input mulch such as municipal compost or chipped bark to prevent any spores being transferred to the leaves above.

In severe cases sulphur sprays or dusts may be used with some success.

Rusts

Rusts are a large group of similar fungi which are almost all host-specific, but attack a wide range of plants. They are all characterized by reddish or brownish pustules on the underside of leaves, which may die back. Plants are rarely killed outright but look very unsightly. Individual spores are short-lived, but produced in vast numbers.

Spores overwinter on dead leaves or in the soil and can persist for several years. Plants which are stressed by drought, waterlogging or high winds are all susceptible.

Grow rust-resistant cultivars wherever possible, but as resistance fades over time, look for new varieties or related species which are immune. Avoid high nitrogen applications, practise long rotations with edible crops and prune out infected growth on ornamentals well below any visible infection as soon as it's seen.

Rake up all diseased foliage and keep soil clear below perennial plants.

Leek rust diminishes with high levels of potash, so non-organic gardeners might like to try applying 2oz (50g) sulphate of potash per sq yd/m to infected plants once or twice in a season, while organic gardeners could incorporate wood ash to the soil in double quantities at fortnightly intervals.

Wilt

Wilt diseases are caused by a variety of organisms but all have similar symptoms, usually caused by a blockage in the plant's sap stream which deprives the leaves above it of water. Asters, the cucurbits, *Clematis*, tomatoes and peonies, among other species, are all affected. Some wilts are host specific, and can persist in the soil for a long time, while others can be spread through transfer of sap, either by sucking insects such as aphids or by pruning tools.

The plant droops, often from the lower leaves first and dies back. If a stem is cut open, even if well above soil level, a dark marking is seen in the centre.

Remove infected stems and destroy: do not compost. In mild attacks, earthing up the unaffected stems with fresh soil so that the plant can form new roots may help. Wash hands and clean tools after touching infected plants.

If replanting, allow a large gap – at least a yard/ metre – between the old and new plants, or dig out and replace the infected soil to a depth of at least 12in (30cm).

There are a number of *Clematis* species which are unaffected by wilt, principally *C. viticella* and its hybrids: in some gardens planting these may be the only option. Annual Aster cultivars 'Milady' and 'Matsumoto' are resistant.

SOME DISEASE RESISTANT VEGETABLE CULTIVARS

Disease	Vegetable	Cultivars
Clubroot	Cabbage	Kilaton F1 Kilaxy F1
	Calabrese	Parthenon
	Cauliflower	Clapton F1
	Swede	Marian Invitation
Common Bean Mosaic Virus	Climbing French bean	Blauhilde Helda Neckar Queen
	Dwarf French bean	Delinel Maxi Opera
	Runner bean	Kelvedon Stringless
Cucumber Mosaic Virus	Climbing French bean	Eva
	Courgette and marrow	Defender Tiger Cross
	Cucumber	Muncher Marketmore

Disease	Vegetable	Cultivars
	Sweet Pepper	Bell Boy Purple Beauty
Downy Mildew	Beetroot	Kestrel F1 Solo
	Lettuce	Balmoral Counter Saladin Tintin
	Pea	Cascadia Jaguar
	Spinach	Medania Scenic F1 Tornado F1
Leek Rust	Leek	Bandit Malabar Porbella Porvite Sultan F1 Zermatt
Parsnip Canker	Parsnip	Cobham Improved Countess F1 Gladiator F1 Marrow Tender and True
Powdery mildew	Beetroot	Solo
	Brussels Sprout	Nautic F1
	Courgette	Firenze F1 Soleil F1
	Cucumber	Burpless Tasty Green La Diva
	Pea	Ambassador Ashton Cavalier Profita
Wilt	Pea	Cascadia Delicata Jaguar

Useful Addresses

Agricultural Network Information Centre (USA)
www.agnic.org

Agroforestry Trust
46 Hunter's Moon, Dartington, Totnes, Devon TQ9 65T, UK
www.agroforestry.org.uk

American Horticultural Society
7931 East Boulevard Drive, Alexandra VA22308, USA
www.ahs.org

Centre for Alternative Technology
Machynlleth, Powys SY20 9A2, UK
01654 705 957
www.cat.org.uk

Chiltern Seeds
Bortree Stile, Ulverston, Cumbria, LA12 7PB, UK.
01229 581137
www.chilternseeds.co.uk

City Farms Urban Agriculture (USA)
www.cityfarmer.org

Common Ground
Gold Hill House, 21 High St, Shaftsbury, Dorset SP7 8JE
01747 850 820
www.commonground.org.uk, and
www.england-in-particular.info

David Austin Roses
Bowling Green Lane, Albrighton, Wolverhampton, WV7 3HB
01902 376 300
www.davidaustinroses.com

Garden Organic (formerly HDRA, Henry Doubleday
Research Organisation)
Ryton Organic Gardens, Coventry CV8 3LG, UK
024 76303 517
www.gardenorganic.org.uk

National Society of Allotment and Leisure Gardeners
(NASALG)
O'Dell House, Hunter's Rd, Corby, Northants, NN17 5JE
01536 266576
www.nasalg.org.uk

Plant Heritage (formerly NCCPG, National Council for the
Conservation of Plants and Gardens)
12 Home Farm, Losely Park, Guilford, Surrey GU3 1HS
01483 447 540
www.nccpg.com

Richter's Herbs
357 Highway 47, Goodwood, Ontario LOC 1A0 Canada
www.richters.com

Rodale Foundation
33, East Minor St, Emmaus PA180098-0099, USA
and
733 Third Avenue, Fifteenth Floor, New York, NY10017 3204
www.rodale.com

The Organic Catalogue
Riverdene, Mosley Road, Hersham, Surrey, Kt12 4RG
0845 1301304
www.OrganicCatalogue.com

Thompson and Morgan Seeds
Poplar Lane, Ipswich, Suffolk, IP8 3BU, UK
01473 695225
www.thompson-morgan.com

Thrive (formerly Horticultural Therapy)
The Geoffery Udal Centre, Trunkwell Park, Beach Hill,
Reading, RG7 2AT
0118 988 5688
www.thrive.org.uk

Thornhayes Nurseries
St Andrews Wood, Dulford, Culompton, Devon EX15 2DF,
UK
01884 266746
www.thornhayes-nursery.co.uk

Waterperry Gardens
Waterperry, near Wheatley, Oxfordshire OX33 1JZ, UK
01844 339226 & 339254
www.waterperrygardens.co.uk

Woodland Trust
Autumn Park, Dysart Road, Grantham, Lincs NG31 6LL, UK
www.woodland-trust.org.uk

Index